her most famous encounter w... door and her family being held...

Paul recalls, "It was a very clear night and the moon was almost full so you had a great view of the night sky. We were in a circle and one of my friends looked up into the stars and noticed this disc-shaped object hovering above us!"

Paul is looking me straight in the eyes and his tone visibly changes to seriousness when he reflects on his experience. "It was a good distance away, it wasn't on top of us, but it was close enough that you could make a clear description of it."

"What did it look like?" "It was silver, and its silhouette was plainly visible. It had three lights with three distinct colors, red, green and white. The craft didn't make a sound. It was completely silent."

"We all noticed it and watched it in amazement. The lights would blink in unison, flashing every so often. We must have watched it for about a minute or two until it...disappeared."

"What do you mean when you say disappeared? How did it disappear?" He paused and said bluntly, "It vanished right before our eyes. We were in an open field and we expected to see this craft shoot off up into the sky, you know? Or off in some direction across the sky. We all still remember this event as clear as day" Paul said.

They all agree that it was something amazing.

What I noticed when driving around this location were the following; next to Betty's original home was a set of large power lines, similar to the ones that run through old Monsterland and Leominster State Forest. Paul mentioned that they used to hang out at an area that was known as the Sand Pits by the power lines. They would all go there and party, have bonfires. Sound familiar? Is it something about these areas that draws the younger locals in or is it the fact that when we are together as a group, our energy attracts something else?

I also noticed that there is a reservoir very close to Betty's first house as well, similar to Leominster State Forest.

I wondered if these reservoirs hold the keys to some of these local mysteries. Time would tell.

Paul's second UFO encounter occurred near the Fitchburg Reservoir in Ashburnham. He was coming back from dinner at a restaurant in Leominster back then called Dan Chan's with his wife.

They were heading back to their home in Ashburnham. As they were driving through the town in a very wooded area they noticed a strange craft hovering above the hillside off to his left.

The craft was shaped like a long, black rectangle. It was very large and it was hovering. It was silent. This bothered Paul. How could something this big be so silent.

Paul immediately pulled the car over to the right of the road to get a better look. He and his wife looked and stared at the strange sight and noticed a small white light that seemed to be centered beneath the craft in the middle.

Then there was a big white flash of light that came from the craft. It blinded the both of them. They looked back at the craft and it was still hovering. Then in a split-second it was gone. It didn't fly away. It just blinked out and disappeared.

When Paul looked back at his wife to talk about the craft vanishing, he noticed that the vehicle was now on the left side of the road! The vehicle was still facing in the same direction but on the other side of the road! How was this possible? They both know that they pulled over to the right side of the road to view the UFO. Then his wife looked down at her watch and she stated that it was odd that they were watching this craft for almost an hour.

"What?! There is no way we were watching that thing for that long! There is no way that was an hour! What the hell?" said a freaked out Paul.

I mentioned he came from dinner in Leominster of all places before this happened. We both laughed.

Paul reluctantly agrees, they had loss of time that they cannot account for. This is a common element of UFO abductions. Paul proclaims that being a hunter, he is always looking and always vigilant. If he sees a big buck at the side of the road, he's going to come back and try to find it. Because of this constant scanning the wood line he noticed the UFO off to the left.

The area where this UFO encounter occurred is hilly, forested and a mix of wide open farmland like space. The area reminds me a lot of some of the different UFO hotspot locations around central Massachusetts.

The very next morning after Paul and his wife's UFO sighting, they received the local Fitchburg Sentinel and Enterprise newspaper, as they do every morning. As Paul's wife is flipping through the newspaper she gets to this big article, this big write up of a local elderly woman claiming to see UFOs near her house and flying out of the Fitchburg reservoir!

This woman had been telling neighbors and anyone that would listen about what she was seeing on her walks...UFOs! She would see them at all times of the day.

The UFOs were small and shaped like a disc and were seen darting in and out of the reservoir. She proclaimed that she has been seeing them for years.

The Fitchburg Reservoir is directly in front of her house, covered by a small section of woods. The view is even better during the fall and winter months when there is no green growth.

The timing of both Paul and his wife seeing a UFO the night before over the hill...and then this UFO article coming out the next morning...in the same area that they had their previous encounter...was incredible. He also tells me that his wife was also one of the original six people for his first UFO sighting! They were married at the time.

That first UFO Paul had seen with his wife was a classic flying saucer and it was about the size of a car. The older woman confirmed that what she was seeing was a small craft as well.

As we were driving over to the next location, Paul confided in me. I think that he feels there might be a connection to his UFO activity with what he was about to share with me.

Every so often, Paul will get this pain in his right side, in his lower back. It is a very uncomfortable pinching feeling. This only seems to occur in the middle of the night. Most accurately around 2am. It will only surface every six months or so, but there hasn't been a definitive pattern to the pain. He would be sound asleep and the pain would wake him up.

The only way that he can alleviate this discomfort is getting up from his bed and going into another room, sitting upright in his recliner for about an hour or so. The pain will finally go away. He doesn't understand this and his doctor did a thorough look over. It only happens once in a great while. It comes and then it goes. The last time he had this occur was about six or seven months ago.

This all started to come about after the second UFO incident. This is also the time frame when these two puncture-type permanent marks appeared on his stomach. They resemble a second pair of nipples but in a different layout. His doctor is equally perplexed by this.

His own personal doctor can't explain what this skin anomaly could be. His wife noticed the marks when they were out swimming together. As Paul got out of the water his wife noticed and commented on the marks. He had no idea where the marks came from. He never thought anything of it again. But these mysterious marks never went away.

Could it be that this lower back pain, these marks on his body are related to these UFO events?

Paul's third UFO encounter was in Gardner, right up the road from his house. He was leaving a friend's residence after a poker game. He was heading down the road when he noticed this enormous white ball of light that engulfed the road in such a way that he couldn't see where the road ended or where it started. He was immediately frightened and couldn't believe how bright it was. It was unlike any vehicle and this light turned the night into daylight.

Paul put the vehicle in reverse and slowly began to accelerate backwards. He noticed that this huge light source started to follow him and move forward towards him.

That's when Paul got really scared and thought of his previous experiences and immediately felt that this was something bad. He slammed the gas pedal and zoomed into a houses' driveway a few feet behind him and slapped the vehicle into drive and gunned it out of the area. He looked back into his rearview mirror and there was nothing there. The white light was gone.

Like Paul's previous two UFO sightings before...the UFO had exited the scene the same way. It just disappeared. Either they are moving away so fast that we can't see them with the naked eye or they may very well be jumping in and out of our dimension.

13

THE YELLOW BOOK

The YELLOW BOOK was mentioned during my meeting with Paul, the experiencer. As stated in the previous chapter he was friendly with one of Betty Andreasson's sons. As Paul and I were driving to the next location on the UFO tour, he asked me to pull over when I brought up the Yellow Book. Sensing he was about to reveal something, I quickly pulled the car off to the side of the road. We got out and walked into the woods a little.

"I knew Betty Andreasson's son really well. Like I told you, I liked Becky so I wanted to visit him as much as possible." We both laughed. One day, Paul went to visit her son at his house. As Paul explained, he typically wouldn't knock. It was customary that Betty's sons' friends could just walk in the door without even a knock or a shout. As most houses were back in the day where your windows were open and your doors were unlocked.

Paul opened the door and he stopped dead in his tracks. There were lit candles placed throughout the room. The shades to the windows were drawn and all of the main lights were off.

Paul says "He was sitting at the kitchen table. He was reading a book. When I came into the room, this "book" was quickly closed and shuffled off to the side and out of my view." Paul thought that the windows being drawn and the candles lit was very strange and then his friends reaction with the book he was reading was even stranger. "Do you think that he purposely moved the book away so that you couldn't see what the book was?" I questioned.

"He quickly pushed the book down onto a chair and out of my view. He didn't want me to see it." He then started talking to Paul with some weird gibberish that didn't sound right. "It was confusing, it was like another language, I wish there was a better way to describe it. It was weird. Then he came out of it after about what seemed like a minute and he began talking normally."

"Did you think while you were experiencing this, standing in front of him while he had this book, that it was some kind of trance he was in? It sounds like he was doing a ceremony or something?"

Paul shakes his head as he recalls being in the Andreasson's home. "I instantly got the sense that something weird was going on. I thought everything was really, well not normal. Things seemed off, way off."

Paul said that the book had a cover on it. Like an old school cover where in grade school you would take a brown grocery bag and make book covers out of them for our school books. "Was there writing on the cover?"

"No. Just a clean, plain brown paper bag. There was no writing on the cover. I remember it being unmarked." "What do you think the book he was reading was?" Paul looked at me and his eyes widened a bit and he smirked.

I realized what Paul was trying to tell me and in not so many words. I stopped Paul during his story before he could even finish. "Wait a second, do you mean to tell me that this book, this book that Betty's son was actually reading was the Yellow Book? The famed YELLOW BOOK?!" Paul looked me straight in the eyes and nodded, "Yes, yes I do." There are those who believe in the reality of this Yellow book and then there are others that believe it to be simply a "disinformation campaign" by an intelligence service associated with the UFO phenomena.

"What do you know about the book?" I asked Paul.

"What I know about "the book" is that it is given to people that have been abducted or are being abducted. They are not to show this book to anyone. There are consequences and they loan out the book for a short period of time before they retrieve it again from the abductees."

From the book, the experiencers are taught where life started and where we go when we die, but they are never ever allowed to show the details of the book to anyone under any circumstances."

Paul said that Betty's son had changed. He changed prior to his two brothers dying in a car crash. And before they died, Paul states that Betty's son was riding his bike everywhere. He never saw him driving a car. All of his friends had cars but him.

Betty Andreasson states that the aliens revealed to her that two of her sons would die in a car crash. If Betty's son was really reading this "Yellow Book" could he have had come to the point where he learned about this? That they would die? It did not claim which sons would die and he chose not to drive a car and use a bicycle instead...to cheat death in a sense? This is just straight up speculation on my part. I would probably do the same.

With that being said, it is believed that the true source of the Yellow Book is from J-Rod, which according to Dan Burisch, a reported worker at Area 51, is a visitor, an alien...from the future. There have been many predictions made by the Yellow Book, a lot that have failed to happen.

Those select few that have read the Yellow Book have put together details for US presidents. This book is called the *Red Book* which began in 1947 and it is updated every five years. It is rumored that details from the Red Book were used by NSA to stop terrorist attacks.

I have often speculated and discussed an idea that I have had about the UFO disclosure movement and how it very well could be more complicated than we truly understand. It could deal with the concept of time itself. Maybe these beings have the ability to stop time like in Betty Andreasson's encounter. The continued reports of missing time with UFO and orb encounters.

We are told by the ancients that time is an illusion. Does the UFO phenomenon and the delay of this disclosure to the public have anything to do with our concept of time and how it can be manipulated? Wouldn't this terrify everyone? These reports and experiences from people seem to imply that this manipulation of time is indeed a possibility.

14

NAVY AND THE NORDICS

What would the Navy have to do with UFOs? Who are the Nordics? The "Yellow Book" may have the answers. There are a lot of UFO researchers who believe that the "Yellow Book", quite often referenced simply as "The Bible" in whispered conversation, does indeed exist. It is a book that is believed to be authored by the aliens themselves. It is the alien's version, their perspective of the history of our universe, detailing the aliens involvement with earth's development and our evolution over the course of time.

There are theories on who was instrumental in obtaining this mysterious book. Since the dawn of the nuclear age there have been rumors persisting that President Eisenhower met with extraterrestrials secretly on several occasions. These meetings took place at Holloman Air Force Base in New Mexico and California. The President's first meeting with the aliens occurred in February of 1954 at the Edwards Air Force Base in California.

The president was on vacation in Palm Springs for several days, because well it was February. Eisenhower would then disappear for several hours not to be seen again until the following morning. The press was told that the Commander-in-Chief had chipped a tooth and was rushed to the dentist, missing a scheduled dinner that evening.

During this missing time, the President reportedly met with two blue-eyed Nordic aliens. It is believed that atomic and nuclear testing by the United States was discussed and we were asked to terminate any continued testing. The official beginning of nuclear testing would occur in New Mexico on July 16th,1945. The earth and nature itself was in jeopardy. The President, a former 5-star general, was unwilling to agree in disarming. (They or another type of alien would meet again a year later.)

Before we jump ahead, I have asked this question before. Could it be that the testing in New Mexico and other locations was affecting not just the earth above ground but maybe the locations of where these Nordic beings live? As above, so below. Could the aliens be hiding from us underground?

The following February, in 1955, a second meeting took place at Holloman Air Force Base in New Mexico. Air Force One landed with about 300 people witnessing the plane taxi to the end of the runway. The pilot then instructed the tower to turn off all radar.

The tower complied and shortly thereafter three round objects were seen in the sky above the base. It has been surmised that radar disrupts the functionality of their craft. It is believed that radar took down the craft that crashed in Roswell, New Mexico in 1947. Turning it off would make sense I believe. This was either a specific request by the aliens or it was simply a way to keep any record of UFOs officially showing up on military radar. If radar is off - then there will be no hit on the radar or a signature of any craft entering the base. A great way to deny this event ever happened.

One of these flying saucers landed next to Air Force One, about 200 feet in front of the President's plane. The other two hovered with one of them disappearing from view. Some say that the second craft went invisible.

The President left Air Force One and walked towards the flying saucer. He was seen shaking the hands of a being at the entrance of the craft and went inside for almost an hour. He emerged from the flying saucer with witnesses recognizing him as the one and only President Eisenhower.

Nine years later in 1964, again at Holloman Air Force Base, three UFOs flew into the area and this time - they were picked up on radar. They also were reportedly filmed. One of the crafts landed and three grayish blue colored beings wearing flight suits were greeted by the base commander and other officers.

It is reported the beings stayed for several days while their craft was repaired. Meetings took place. Researchers state an exchange was made and agreement was signed between us and them. We would receive their technology and help in advancing ahead and they would get the opportunity to abduct people, plucking them from their homes as they sleep. Who they took for these abductions was this agreed upon? I question was this the meeting when we were given the Yellow Book? Could it also contain the list of abductees that were targeted?

Before you say "no way", a retired New Hampshire state representative, Henry McElroy Jr. claims to have seen a secret briefing document which was intended for President Eisenhower. By way of a video announcement, which you can find on YouTube, McElroy states that this secret document contained information that the aliens were in the US and the President could meet with them. It is believed this was the catalyst for the initial meeting between Eisenhower and the Nordic aliens.

This leads to so many other rumblings about things like there being two crashes not one at Roswell, New Mexico. As well as an exchange program of US astronauts and gray aliens called ebens under *Project Serpo*. Many theorists believe that Steven Spielberg's movie, *"Close Encounters of the Third Kind"* was inspired by the Holloman landing. If you have seen the film then you know how it ends with star Richard Dreyfuss leaving with the aliens. This ending was the beginning of Project Serpo but instead there were really ten passengers from our side who left.

Could there be multiple versions of this Yellow book? It is reported that the original book was indeed gifted to the US government at the famous Holloman AFB landing which occurred in April of 1964. The book is reportedly a fiberglass-like material that is 2 and ½ inches thick and transparent with a bright yellow border, hence its name.

The reader will begin by looking at the transparent surface of this book and this will activate images and text. The activation of the book by an individual's eye or retina is what we know of today as biometric scanning. There are several members of the military and others that have said that they have seen this book. Stating "it would take a lifetime to read it and another lifetime to understand it."

This Yellow Book contains historical stories, photographs of our universe, details of the writers. These were the Ebens and their former world and other strange stories pertaining to our universe, earth's history and our distant past. What we know as looking like the gray aliens. It is reported that there are holographic images that are projected from the book and one of them is the crucifixion of Jesus Christ. The aliens state that Jesus was...an alien.

There was a Brazilian psychic medium by the name of Chico Xavier. He had the ability to communicate with multidimensional beings and spirits. They would give him predictions. So much so that when he passed away in 2002 at the age of 92 he had written over 500 books! These books were written using his gift of psychography which allows one to access spiritual information and channel those into words. One of these predictions that was received was concerned with alien contact.

There was an agreement between the intergalactic council on the day that Neil Armstrong stepped onto the moon. If we did not annihilate the earth over the next fifty years starting from July 20, 1969, the day we landed on the moon, we would finally have alien interaction. This is supposed to happen by July 2019. It is July 19th as I write this. As I am sure with most prophecies, this one will not happen either.

One of these aliens they speak of is Jesus Christ. He was an alien and he is part of this intergalactic council. He came down to earth two thousand years ago to show us the ways of love and peace.

Could the UFO mystery somehow envelop time travel, time warps and the reality that this is something that we might not be ready to deal with as a race? That UFOs are indeed time travelers? Are the craft themselves - time travel machines?

An anthropologist who specializes in UFO studies thinks so. Professor, Dr. Michael P. Masters of Montana Tech recently penned a book entitled *Identified Flying Objects* on the theory of time traveling aliens. He believes that all of the UFO sightings over the past hundred years or more are encounters with time travelers.

Humanoid beings with incredible technology, taking people from their homes, their vehicles, implants...and missing time. We are being studied. He calls these beings "extra-tempestrials". They are our distant human descendants coming back in time to review our present, their distant past.

Due to our accelerated technological growth and

advancement Dr. Masters believes that it is just a matter of time before we have achieved the ability to time travel.

I believe we may already have.

15

MERGING DREAMS

My daughter Aysia had a dream that she felt was all too real. This dream was in the middle of other dreams she had during the night. This one, however, was more vibrant than the rest. She was outside on the grass, then the earth swallowed her up like a sinkhole. She started to go down like on a waterslide.

She was able to see that it was dark, black and colors were emanating down the tube as she went. As she was falling, she states that it felt like she was falling for a very long time. She was seeing colors in the tube. The colors of the rainbow. She then fell into a ball pit of sorts. It didn't feel like rubber balls, but she felt that it was the consistency of a cloud-like texture.

There are a lot of people in this area that resembles a train station after she exits the ball pit. A place where people are coming and going. She didn't see a train, but that was the feeling she was receiving about this place. Like a soul depository. When she started to walk forward it seemed like it was taking forever. There were people around that were always moving and when she tried to look at their faces they would turn.

Aysia continued to walk forward which seemed to be never ending. She then spots a robot-like figure or being. It was holding up a sign. The sign had her name on it. The way the sign was projecting her name was one letter at a time. A...Y...S...I...A. Like the Goodyear Blimp advertising scroll. She stopped at the robot. It was silver with a bluish tint. It was like a hi-tech cartoon-shaped, but the technology looked advanced. She said it was as if it was trying to look less advanced by looking more like a cartoon or an older version of a robot like seen in early television.

Unlike the other people around her in this "dream" the robot was in her vision the entire time as she was walking forward. It didn't change like the others. She had perfect vision of the robot and when people were walking across her vision, their bodies would contort in a way to avoid interrupting her vision of the robot in front of her path. As if they knew she had to see this robot continually. She remarked that it took what seemed like hours to get to the robot.

Once Aysia got to the robot and realized that it was her name. "That's my name." Aysia felt a low vibrational frequency when encountering this robot - it wasn't a warm and fuzzy feeling. The waves were hitting her body. She had this same feeling when she awoke from the dream. She said that the robot resembled a combination of "Rosie from The Jetsons" and Karen the robot from Spongebob Squarepants.

Both cartoon personifications of a robot. It didn't say anything to her. The robot was now holding a two-sided sign...there was a name on the other side. On the opposite side was another girl. She was standing directly in front of the robot in such a way that she was hidden from Aysia's view until Aysia leaned forward. Aysia realized that it was her sister Lena. Lena didn't have time to respond or react - Aysia awoke from her dream.

Aysia said the feeling she had through her body reminded her of being stung by a bee or getting some sort of an electric shock. Aysia said that she has had only a handful of vivid dreams in her early life but this is one of those dreams that occured four years ago and it sticks in her mind almost like it happened yesterday.

Aysia, slowly waking up, goes through her normal routine. She makes a bowl of cereal and sits down on the couch to watch television before heading off to school. Lena enters the room and begins to tell her about her dream that she just had. Lena goes on to describe the same ball pit, the same quicksand feeling of being sucked down into this lower world. Aysia's eyes widen.

Lena would then explain that she noticed a robot, with the same description mind you as Aysia's dream, holding a blinking sign with her name...L...E...N...A. Lena would eventually approach the robot. This robot had two sides. On the other side was Aysia's name and Aysia standing there and awaiting next steps. Aysia noticed another girl in her dream on the other side of the robot. It was her sister Lena! They both started to freak out as they told me about their incredible *shared* dream. Where were they in the dream? Was this dream world real?

16

THE WHITE WOLF

After attending a conference called *Experiencers Speak - Enlightened Ones Expo* in Portland, Maine in 2016, I had an interesting experience. It was late August, so the summer heat was in full swing. The next day, back at home, I worked in the yard all day cleaning it up. It was hot and I had removed my shirt due to the intense heat. That evening, as the sun was about to set, something landed on my bare back as I made my way onto my porch.

I quickly reached behind me and grabbed this winged creature from my back, bringing it to my face for closer inspection. To my surprise, a brownish colored praying mantis with jet black eyes stared back at me. I was startled. My wife Amy quickly grabbed an old pickle jar from inside and we placed the mantis inside.

Once secured, we made a few holes with a hammer and nail and planned to show it to the kids and then let it go. This was a pivotal moment for me. This praying mantis struck a weird chord of intrigue within me. I wanted to know what the spiritual significance was with this insect. It was like a nagging thought that persisted. So I finally looked.

The praying mantis is the oldest symbol of God. To people of southern Africa, he is a trickster God, a shapeshifter known as Kaggen. A demi-urge, a god-like creator and a figure of folklore responsible for fashioning and maintaining the physical universe. These creatures are often seen when major internal and external life changes are taking place. The brown praying mantis is the symbol of earth and all its colors. It is the totem animal of Chinese Kung Fu and is also known as a spiritual warrior. The praying-mantis symbolism also includes calmness, stillness, focus, and concentration.

I searched further to discover the meaning of having one of these insects land on you. I couldn't believe I was reading this. "The praying-mantis spirit totem is a sign of good luck. When it lands on you, expect to experience luck in big and small forms." A praying mantis landing on you is a sure sign that it has and always has been your spirit animal. It has the special ability to seek and receive answers from the unknown. The word "mantis" is derived from the Greek "mantikos" which means prophet.

The praying mantis delves into the mystical realm of spirit and is often seen as a spirit guide. It is also the symbol of meditation. Its message is often associated with having a calm, peaceful and still mind so that you can truly focus on your intention and what you must do to make it happen. The mantis always has its intention and nothing can stop what it wants to do.

I interpreted this brown praying mantis landing on me as some sort of message or communication from the universe. I reached out to conference organizer Audrey "StarChild" Hewins about this experience. She told me that there were praying mantis flying around everywhere at the previous year's event. This affirmed my belief that this was a message from the universe.

However, if I was not seeking, not looking to see what the hidden meaning could be, I would have missed the message. I would have been blind to the fact that someone was trying to get my attention. From that point forward, I looked at animals on the physical plane as messengers as well as the ones I would encounter in the dream world.

Dreams have been an important aspect of my life from childhood to today. They have been extremely vivid and a good portion of them are what I would refer to as feeling "real".

Is it simply chemical reactions taking place or are our brains processing different events, concerns or problems from the day and dreams are just a way for our brains to decipher and calculate or arrive at a solution?

Dreams have been the root of human milestones. Songs, films and books are written based on dreams. Inventions and discoveries have been made all due to dreams. My son Noah once asked me, "Dad, do you ever wonder if dreams are the real world and the world we are living in is a dream?" I told him, "Yes, quite a few times. Like right now." He was seven at the time.

I am able to remember quite a few dreams, so much so, that I started to make a game out of remembering them and where my subconscious might have provided the story line. When I would wake, I was able to recall times during the previous day when I might have said something that triggered a part of the dream that evening. Or maybe I heard or saw something from a movie that I could place as the culprit materializing in my dream.

There are some dreams however, that not only seem more colorful than real life, but actually feel more real, like we are in some other dimension or plane. When you start paying attention to your dreams, really honing in on the details and get vivid and lucid so that you are conscious in your dreams, that's when things get interesting.

Native American cultures have always revered the dream world, believing it to be in fact more than a dream - it's a dreamworld - and it is real. It's a place that is considered to be a true reality, another plane of existence. They also consider animals to be sacred and the ones that show up in your dream world are trying to tell you something. Your totem animals, your spirit animals are here to guide you. Native American's stressed the importance of the animals that appear in your dreams and in your visions are ones that should be acknowledged and observed.

"Your soul dreams those dreams; not your body, not your mind. Those dreams come true. The soul travels all over the world when you dream."

- Chippewa elder John Thunderbird

Several years ago when I was looking for work, I was in preparation for a job interview in Boston. I spent a good amount of time trying to research the company. After a while, I wasn't sure what the company really did. The website was almost cryptic and it was a company name I wasn't familiar with, but they were on a posh street in downtown Boston and on the top floor. They were hiring and I needed a job. It wasn't a matter of whether or not they were legit, something about it made me feel uncomfortable. I was getting what you would call "a weird vibe" when I would think or focus on this company.

That evening I had an interesting dream. In my dream I was walking down a hiking trail. There were woods all around and the trail was a dirt one with decent size rocks. The terrain to the right seemed steep, almost like a slightly steep ravine. I was alone. At least it seemed that way when suddenly a white wolf appeared on the path in front of me.

I stopped dead in my tracks. It was maybe ten yards or so away from me and it was directly in my path. It was stopped and staring at me. The wolf was big and majestic. I sensed a male energy from it and its coat was so white that it was rich looking. The eyes of the wolf were blue as the ocean and amongst the white fur mesmerizing to look at.

I felt threatened. This wolf didn't seem to be friendly. It showed its teeth. I quickly turned to my left and noticed a short, but thick branch on the ground. It was small enough to hold in one hand but big enough to become protection if need be. I looked at the wolf and then at the branch. I took a breath and then I snatched it up as quickly as I could all the while glancing back and forth from the branch to the wolf. The wolf's eyes were hooked onto the branch. Then its eyes were back on me. It didn't growl. It just stared. It didn't feel like a good stare. It wanted something.

I placed the branch in my right hand and lifted it up above my head, motioning to the wolf with a forward motion repeatedly as if I was about to throw it. When the wolf didn't move, I threw the branch in the wolf's direction but towards the right and it went tumbling down the ravine. The wolf swiftly followed suit and ensued chase after the branch. The threat was momentarily avoided and I was back on the trail alone with no wolf in sight.

I woke up and quickly wrote down the dream. I wasn't sure what the meaning of the wolf was. Was this my totem animal? As a child, this was an animal that was easily my favorite. I even used to sign my name like I was signing an autograph and I would pencil in a wolf paw below the signature.

Was this dream trying to tell me something? It was very vivid and real and it stayed with me all day. I couldn't seem to shake the significance of the wolf. A white wolf with blue eyes. I had to get ready for my interview.

I arrived at the location of my interview. It was in a high rise building in the business district and my meeting was on the top floor. I got off the elevator and was met by a secretary and had me take a seat. A few minutes later I was taken to a lavish waiting room which was in the center of the office building. Afghan rugs and expensive paintings decorated the room. There were two hefty leather chairs that were positioned so that they were facing each other. I was ushered to one of the chairs and I sat down. "Wait right here, I will get the hiring manager. He's excited to meet with you."

I met with the hiring manager who I had spoken with over the phone. He was visibly stressed out. He looked like he hadn't slept in a day or so and was sweating profusely during the interview. When I would ask particular questions he wouldn't fully answer them and left things somewhat vague.

I was getting an uneasy feeling about the whole thing as I had while doing research on the company. Then he said, "Our CEO would love to meet with you. Let me get him really quick." A few minutes go by and I am feeling really uneasy now, to the point that I know this job isn't going to work out for me. The pay sucks, the travel, the job itself sounds awful. I was starting to consider just getting up and walking out of the interview when in comes the CEO.

I lost my breath. He reaches out his hand to greet me. I stand up and shake his hand. He sits down directly across from me and it hit me like a crashing wave on my face. The CEO is wearing a white - neatly pressed - dress shirt with cufflinks. His hair is as white as snow and his eyes...a piercing blue. Here he is sitting across from me, smiling and staring me down and I realize at that very moment that this is the wolf that I dreamed about. The white wolf with the blue eyes. I remember that I looked for a stick or a branch during my dream and I threw the wolf off of my path. I knew that at this very moment, this job wasn't for me.

17

PROTECTORS OF THE PORTAL

I read this article which came out two days ago via *The Oregonian,* July 2, 2019 (on World UFO Day no less), talking about how iconic author Peter Matthiessen was a Bigfoot devotee.

Matthiessen not only believed in sasquatch, he saw one, and coming from an intelligent and influential literary figure, one should maybe ponder the possibility of what this thing could be.

He won the National Book award three times. His works include "*Shadow Country*", "*In the Spirit of Crazy Horse*" and "*The Snow Leopard*". Passing away in 2014, he is considered one of the greatest modern nature writers in the lyrical tradition. He co-founded Paris Review, a literary journal.

Matthiessen's nephew, Jeff Wheelwright, a writer as well, is doing some research into his uncle's Bigfoot obsession that has been known to only a few. Wheelwright is writing an essay for *Yale Review*. What he uncovered is incredible.

In 1976, while Peter Matthiessen was in the Pacific Northwest, he saw "a tall, bipedal figure run across the road, and disappear into the trees. It jumped a tangle of stumps and logs with the ease of a deer."

Peter's obsession with Bigfoot was such that he struggled with writing a book about the subject for over thirty years, being the last work on his desk when he took his last breath. While hiking through Nepal in 1973, an experience he recounts in his book "The Snow Leopard", he became more fascinated with the subject of Sasquatch. He then attended a Bigfoot conference in British Columbia and befriended monster hunter Peter Byrne.

Prior to all of this...Peter Matthiessen was an undercover CIA agent. Peter was a longtime devotee of Zen Buddhism. Stilling the mind. He's an outdoorsman and believed that Bigfoot very may well indeed by some kind of shape-shifting creature.

The Kushtakas, as sasquatch is known in Native cultures in Alaska, are believed to have the ability to shape-shift and mimic the screams of women and children. Looking like half-otter, half-man, there are stories of them luring men to their deaths.

He believed in an African shapeshifting legend about a "marauding hyena". When it was finally killed, it was found on the ground...as a human corpse.

On April 9th, 2019, Yeti tracks were discovered by the Indian Army Mountaineering Expedition Team, measuring 32 by 15 inches long! Those measurements are extraordinary, especially for the Yeti's reported short stature when it comes to height.

The tracks were found near the Makalu Base Camp, which is a remote mountainous area between Nepal and Tibet. The team shared their photographic evidence of the enormous tracks three weeks after the discovery by means of a Tweet to their enormous twitter following.

"This elusive snowman has only been sighted at Makalu-Barun National Park in the past," the army added along with images of what it claimed were tracks from the mythical Himalayan monster also known as the Abominable Snowman.

Motherboard spoke with Ross Barnett, an author and paleogeneticist who matched alleged Yeti hair samples back in 2014, with that of a type of Himalayan brown bear.

"Without good photos it would be foolhardy to discount the footprints as being from a snow leopard or a brown bear, animals that are known to live in the region."

With the tracks being found near the Nepal/China border, the Nepal Army couldn't stand the social media attention and like a Kardashian - they went off - claiming that the Indian Army simply had found the tracks of a bear. The Nepal Army went to the location only to turn up empty...the tracks like their social media dreams....were gone.

The Nepal Army claimed to have spoken with the locals when they investigated the sighting. The locals stated that "strange tracks" are typically found in the area...but they are just bears.

Wildlife experts agree. These "yeti" tracks were simply bear prints expanded to a larger size by the sun's heat and wind only to become larger than life going viral on social media and even making NBC news. Bear. Sun. Melting. Done. Case closed?

There is a history of this creature and there are more recent sightings. It is possible the locals are protecting a creature in their homeland.

Yeti—a Sherpa word for "wild man" got some serious press back in 1951. A British explorer named Eric Shipton, looking for an alternative route up Mt. Everest, found a footprint that appeared to be hominoid. He took a picture and the rest is history.

But the Yeti goes back before the Eric Shipton "Yeti footprint" photo and with a throw back into pre-19th century.

According to H. Siiger, the Yeti was a part of the pre-Buddhist beliefs of several Himalayan peoples. He was told that the Lepcha people worshipped a "Glacier Being", resembling the yeti, as a "God of the Hunt".

He also reported that followers of the Bön religion once believed the blood of the "mirgod" or "wild man" had use in certain mystical ceremonies. The being was depicted as an apelike creature who carries a large stone as a weapon, making a whistling swoosh sound.

These "wild men" may have a greater purpose. Could the locals be protecting these "bears" from the rest of the world because these creatures are here to protect something special?

Ready to go down the rabbit hole...or rather a portal of sorts?

18

SUPERNATURAL SASQUATCH

The Bon religion speaks of the entrance of "Shambala" or "Olmo Lungring" being guarded by wild mythical beasts. Many have surmised that these beasts may in fact be the Yeti and the area in and around Mt. Kailash in the Himalayas is this sacred land and entrance that is being protected by these beings.

Olmo Lungring or Shambala, is said to be an imperishable sacred land. It is believed to be the spiritual center of the world, also being referred to as containing "The Great White Lodge" which existed on earth from the very beginning of the human race. Inhabited by ascended masters, it is said to be imperishable because it exists on another dimension.

A place where the celestial gods of clear light descended from heaven to earth taking up the form of humans, their physical bodies having been prepared for their ensoulment.

This land at the center of this mystery has been known by various names and spoken about in different ancient traditions. It is said to be the land of the Vidyadharas beyond the Himalayas, spoken of in the Puranas and other ancient books of India.

"In ancient and medieval times, and even in modern times, there have been persistent rumors of a secret brotherhood of enlightened beings or Vidyadharas, possessing great knowledge and power, who, in a remote corner of Central Asia, preserve the Ancient Wisdom which was revealed at the very beginning of the human race."

This secret invisible plane of existence contains a hidden library of sorts containing the highest mystical teachings from the heavenly realm. It is a land that is only accessible by those that are considered "siddhas" or "awakened ones". It is claimed at the end of the world this special land will rise up and merge with the heavens.

It is believed that the knowledge that is contained in Shambala is the precise knowledge of who we really are, where we have come from and where we go, known as the Supreme Secret.

There very well may be a portal or entrance to this special place at the foot of Mt. Kailash. Areas that are considered to contain portals - like Monsterland for example - have Bigfoot reports within and around the area.

These areas are considered sacred by Native Americans having high energy with connections to greater ley lines of energy. A grid of energy lines that envelop the entire planet.

Could bigfoot and the yeti be protecting and guarding these sacred areas of energy throughout the world? There is a growing theory that Bigfoot/Sasquatch and the different types like the Yeti or Yowie are indeed not Gigantopithecus, a physical creature, but an interdimensional being.

Something that is half-spirit / half - matter.

The Mukleshoot tribe in Washington state contend that one should never say their name or even think of sasquatch, this will only draw them to you. Never whistle at night as this is one of the ways that they communicate with others. They also have the power to render a human unconscious with just a simple touch!

Although we don't often hear of stories of sasquatch attacking humans, aside from rare accounts like Ape Canyon in 1924, where a group of miners had reportedly killed a sasquatch by shooting one only to have their cabin attacked that evening from multiple ones retaliating for the loss of one of their own. The miners quickly left the area leaving all of their equipment behind. When we dig deeper into the stories of the indigienous people of North America, there are indeed stories of sasquatch attacking Native Americans.

In the traditions of many Salish and Northwest indian tribes, Stick Indians, is another name for Bigfoot within the tribes. They are described as being forest spirits, extremely dangerous ones that have the ability to hypnotize, paralyze or even cause insanity in humans. They will laugh or whistle to entice humans whether that be children, women or men who enter the woods at night. Described as large and hairy these Stick Indians have been said to kidnap or eat people. There are smaller ones that are considered forest dwarves by the Cayuse and Yakama tribes.

These stories of magical beings, physical in appearance, yet disappearing or appearing to be supernatural have been recorded for hundreds of years. Although it is so strange and science fiction in scope upon first glance - this creature needs our attention. The Yeti may very well be something out of this world.

The Clackamas tribe calls sasquatch Skookum or mountain devil. They believe that they are a tribe-like people. They have a legend that says that before sasquatches can become an "adult" they have to pass a test. This test requires them to jump in front of a human on a trail and wave their hands in front of the human's face without being seen. This must be done three times!

If true - just think of all the times you have been hiking in the woods and something could have been right in front of your face and you didn't even know it.

Many indigenoius traditions throughout the world, mythology and oral traditions describe sasquatch like creatures living close by to them in some cases as a monster.

In Kathy Moskowitz Strain's book, *Giants, Cannibals & Monsters: Bigfoot in Native Culture,* she describes stories from the Pacific Northwest tribes that speak of these creatures living very close to them and interacting with them but always separate. The "other tribe" would have less skill set with tools and other items like canoes or fishing line.

They were known as tricksters, stealing things was common throughout Native American history. They were known to steal fish-nets, canoes and tools. Items often times returned, but broken.

These creatures were also known to throw sticks and rocks, similar to sasquatch behavior. They have also been known to steal food but to also gift humans. They will leave rocks or sticks behind as gifts. Also known as stick glyphs - similar to a type of sign language or hieroglyphics.

One of these early stories of gifting is with the Modoc tribe of central Oregon. They call the sasquatch *Matah Kagmi.* They are considered very shy and will avoid man, only coming out at night. Their homes are in deep burroughs in the mountainside.

One of the Native American elders of the tribe came upon a strange looking bush that had a strong odor. As he got closer and upon further inspection, he realized that he was looking at something covered head to toe in thick coarse hair. As he got even closer it began to cry out making the sound like "Nyyaaaah!" then "Aaagooouuumm!" and he knew that it was at Matah Kagmi.

He made a gesture of friendship towards the creature and offered his fish on a line he caught. A few days later he heard the same strange sounds from the creature a few days before just outside his cabin. When he came outside he saw that there was a gift left for him. It was a deer skin, wood for fuel, berries and other food.

Author Kathy Moskowitz Strain is also a scientist. She works with the Native American tribes in California, as a manager for tribal relations. She holds a Masters Degree in Anthropology from California State University. She has had her own experience seeing not one, but four sasquatch in the Pacific Northwest.

She was with a group of five people who were out doing an investigation for several days looking for evidence of sasquatch. They were at a location in Oklahoma where there had been a lot of recent bigfoot activity. Kathy and other researchers were staying out in cabins during the month of May. They had rocks thrown at the roof of one of the cabins at night. They all went out to investigate.

They got together in a semicircle after checking around the cabins for the culprit when all of the sudden Kathy notices these two figures, a small one and a larger one running straight for the group. She yelled, "There they are!" Kathy began to run at the creatures!

When Kathy changed the pursuit, running towards the figures, Kathy states "they bolted up the hillside...like..I can't even tell you how fast it was. The smaller one was four feet and the bigger one about six feet. They were a dark brown, black color." Kathy was astonished at how fast these creatures could run and move. She had a meltdown afterwards because Kathy was shocked how close they were and she could have been hurt. She was overcome with fear and agrees that these are the apex predator in our woods. She doesn't believe that they are human, but that they are an unclassified and undiscovered animal. She believes that they are definitely an animal but with no supernatural abilities.

19

BIGFOOT GETS VISUAL

Les Stroud, known for his *Survivorman* series, where he is alone, living in different parts of the world, decided to do a series of shows entitled *Survivorman: Bigfoot*. His first experience with something out of place was when he was filming in Alaska for his series *Survivorman* in 2009 and heard the sound of grunting that Les would say equated to that of a primate or ape.

Louder and deeper, the sound reverberated through Les's chest, then it took off running and ripped through the forest. This didn't happen in the middle of the night, this was during the middle of the day. This experience led Les to do a new series focused on Bigfoot and inserting himself this time not only in the wilds looking for Sasquatch, but with different researchers on different ends of the Bigfoot spectrum if you will. People that believe that Bigfoot is indeed a long lost animal yet to be discovered, and others that believe that it is an alien.

During one of the episodes, Les was visiting a UFO hotspot and was on the top of the mountain. He spotted lights that were hovering, bigger than a Concorde, that just disappeared out of thin air. Later that night, while Les was sleeping in his sleeping bag, he felt some presence or figure leaning in and on top of him. He knew that he wasn't dreaming, something was in the tent with him.

Les also left out food, and candy bars, which were bait for Bigfoot. They set up an infrared camera that was focused on the bait. The food disappeared and the camera, which should have been tripped and would have photographed the culprit, showed nothing. The food vanished as if by some sort of ghost. He also revealed that there was "mindspeak" between him and a sasquatch in the Great Smokey Mountains of Tennessee.

He heard a huge voice in his head. 'We are right over here. Two hills away from you. If you want to see us...stay." Les replied that he wasn't ready for this. He was not ready to engage with these beings. He now questions what it is he is really tackling out there.

TOM

Just west of Leominster State Forest a local resident was experiencing something that he described as resembling drones. Tom has a spectacular view of the state forest as well as the area along Route 2, which runs alongside Leominster State Forest. He began to notice these strange ball of lights - white lights - flying along the path of Route 2 towards his house. He would witness a light and not far behind there was another one. Slow and steady with no navigational lights and no blinking lights.

They would fly low above the trees in the back of his house. He became concerned when one of these drones was seen flying close enough to his house to warrant a phone call to the police department. These lights seemed to be making an ongoing appearance by his residence and close enough to look inside his windows. When I asked him if he remembers hearing any noise being emitted from these lights when they would make their way next to his home. They were silent. He described the lights or drones as being shaped like a diamond and about the size of your average house door. That's big for a drone.

There was a UFO sighting reported near Tom, although the exact date has not been established in the report, around this time frame when Tom was seeing these drones. Both sightings are in close proximity to one another but not in the same town. Tom has stated that he sees them throughout the year.

On March 21, 2019, a UFO report was made to NUFORC. Two attorneys, a boyfriend and girlfriend had just arrived home in the neighboring town of Boylston. As they were pulling into the garage, the couple noticed a top or diamond-shaped object hovering motionless in the sky. There seemed to be an aura, an energy field or fog around the object. It didn't have clearly defined edges and looked fuzzy.

All around the object appeared to be lightning of different colors arching and flashing randomly. Red. Green. Blue. There was a sense of dead silence. No sound was coming from the craft. No noticeable sound around them. It stayed in the same spot in the sky for what seemed like a long time. It didn't move from its position until it slowly began to drift, heading southwest.

The couple then witnessed two fast moving lights with a jet-like sound coming from the east by northeast direction, which the witnesses believe is the same direction of a local Air Force Base. When the boyfriend looked back in the direction of where the object was hovering - it was gone. The jets now approached and came directly into the same airspace that the diamond-shaped object was hovering before it disappeared.

They never saw the craft leave. This craft fits the same description as the one seen by Tom. Tom made a call to the local police department to file a formal complaint. Tom became so upset with these "drones" he exclaimed to a police officer that he will shoot one down if it shows up around his house again. "I don't need people looking into my windows at night!" The police assured him that no one would be shooting any drones down. Tom would be harming personal property if that was the case. Tom told them to send a cruiser down to his house right now as they were flying around his neighborhood as they spoke. They sent an officer down to take a look.

When the police officer arrived, Tom took the officer to the location of where he has been seeing the drones. Not too long after the officer arrived, one of these drones was heading straight towards the house. The police officer removed his flashlight and both Tom and the officer, standing side by side, while he had his flashlight on the object, watched as the oncoming "drone" flew over Tom's house.

They both looked at each other immediately. The first thing that dawned on Tom is that it made NO sound. It was completely silent. The officer then remarked that this was no drone. It was silent. The description of the drone from Tom is that this is shaped like a diamond and it is about the size of a door. There was a light on either side of the craft and one in the middle. One thing that stood out in the description of the craft by Tom was this, it had no weld marks. It was seamless. This is a description that often describes flying saucers. There is an absence of any sign of molding it's as if the craft is made of one piece.

There was talk that the officer had had some experiences with UFOs in the past, since childhood. I would come to learn that Tom also had what some would refer to as a "screen memory". A screen memory is one that is almost like a new film has been edited into your memory bank. So instead of an event being replayed in your mind that "someone" doesn't want you to remember or experience, a screen memory is put in its place to fill that gap, once the real memory has somehow been removed. Like what I talked about in the UFO in LA Chapter.

Tom remembers when he and his sister were young, he was about 5 or 6, that a red, white and blue hot air balloon landed in their backyard. His sister, who was with him in the memory, doesn't remember this happening. This is reminiscent of a screen memory.

But of course, I had to ask if his sister had any experiences with UFOs. She told me that she did. A daylight sighting. She was at work in Leominster and she was on the second floor of her company's building. The room that they were in was surrounded by huge glass windows. It was wide open and has an amazing view of the landscape.

It was a gorgeous sunny day. There were some clouds but visibility was great. She was discussing something with her co-worker when out of the corner of her eye she notices this strange craft. It was shaped like a rectangle and was all black and it was big. She said that she mentioned the huge box looking thing to her co-worker and they just watched it slowly fly through the sky, through clouds but low enough to see that it wasn't a plane and she remarked that what was so odd was how slow it was moving. Now this wasn't a blimp. There have been descriptions of this type of rectangle craft before.

When I asked her what happened to the craft. She paused for a few moments and said that she wasn't sure. She can't remember. They noticed it, watched it and then she thinks that they went back to discussing their original conversation. She has no recall of seeing it disappear - just losing interest and getting back to work.

When someone has had a UFO experience, I tend to dive right into their backstory, their childhood. "Did you have any weird paranormal experiences when you were growing up? Did you have any previous UFO sightings before this one? Tom's experiences and encounters with strange drones flying over his house was brand new to him and there was something not normal about this area that he residing in now.

He's only been living at this home for a few years. Another interesting aspect is that when he would be on the phone or he was listening to music in the house, there would be strange interference and weird sounds coming through on their house phone when these "drones" would pass by their house. They made the connection when they noticed this happening upon the appearance of these strange craft.
I gave him a copy of my book *Monsterland* and told him to start reading.

There might be some answers for him but also, I had an ulterior motive. When people have read my first book, they have talked about having old memories unlocked from their subconscious. Remembering experiences that would be described as being UFO abduction experiences, UFO sightings or strange cryptid encounters.

I felt that there was more to Tom and his history. He started reading *Monsterland* and I told him that when he is outside and he is seeing these orbs or strange balls of light, to use his mind to reach out to them. He looked at me funny initially as anyone would if you made this type of request. I told him that there is a thought connection, a way to communicate with these lights, beings or craft.

I told him to try it and see what happens. I didn't expect to hear what happened next. Tom began to read the book and when he went outside at night and looked into the night sky, he started to beckon the lights to come his way. He truly wanted to find out what they hell these things were.

Tom had several more of these sightings and had the chance to take a picture of one of the craft. There are no lights on the craft. It seemed to be crescent-shaped.
Again, Tom heard no sound emanating from the craft. It was completely silent. A friend commented that these were

classified government drones. He had a source. When I told him about the latest update from my colleague and it being a possible explanation for these drones, Tom seemed relieved. Could they, whoever they are, be working on silent drone technology and testing it around private property? Possibly.

Here's where it gets weird. Real weird.

I told Tom that there is a connection to these balls of light, these orange orbs that keep popping up in our neck of the woods. They are connected to Sasquatch. He was open-minded to this concept but wasn't sure how. I told him that by reading the book some of these questions would be answered.

In the midst of all this strangeness Tom woke up at 3am. He couldn't sleep. He was tossing and turning so he decided to get up and head outside. He walked into his backyard and was rearranging one of his lawn sprinklers when he got the feeling that he was being watched.

He looked over in the direction of a telephone pole along his street. His gaze was correctly positioned because out from behind the telephone pole a creature peeked out and looked at him. They made eye contact. He couldn't believe it. It was a bigfoot, about six to seven feet tall, covered in black hair. Tom dropped the sprinkler head and just looked in awe as the creature then took off across the street in two big steps.

The creature then jumped over a stone wall made a few more steps and then stopped. Tom heard the pads of the feet slap on top of the asphalt as it made its way across the street. Tom was astonished at the speed of this creature. It was on two legs. It was hairy and it scared the hell out of him.

Tom told me that he felt that once it cleared the road and jumped the stone wall, it made a few steps and he felt that it was looking back at him again, standing motionless in the dark woods. Tom had seen enough and was terrified. He ran back inside the house.

That morning for whatever reason, I posted a picture of the Pennsylvania trail camera bigfoot photo on my *Monsterland Podcast's* Instagram account. It is the one where a creature is bending down to pick up something. When you see the image, it looks odd. There are black bears in the other trail camera pictures and this one is a different color. If you take the time and compare them, there is a two-legged creature with a cone-shaped head and a hunchback-type stance in their midst.

This picture freaked Tom out so much because this was exactly what he had seen! I didn't talk to him about his sighting until later in the day, after I had posted this image. Tom couldn't believe it.

Tom said that this image was an exact replica of what he had seen earlier that morning! He described it as a chimpanzee-like creature with a hunchback.

This image is by hunter Rick Jacobs, which you can find with a quick internet search. It shows a bigfoot, in my opinion, caught by a trail camera with an automatic trigger. Located in Pennsylvania's Allegheny National Forest, Jacobs captured the image of this creature on September 16th, 2007.

Thanks to this hunter's camera some people believe it could be a sasquatch, or bigfoot. Others say it's just a bear with a bad skin infection. I believe this is the real deal when you see the other photos which show black bears and the comparison is noticeable.

When I look at this image - I see a Sasquatch bending over to pick something up. The hind legs look much longer than a bear's legs. It also looks like you can make out the side profile of a face, with a cone head shape. It looks like something that is standing on two legs that is bending down rather than something being four-legged.

To summarize for a moment, Tom has drones flying over his house, he starts to spend more time looking out at the stars at night to see if he could see these strange lights again. He's not thinking UFOs. He's thinking drones - as anyone would initially. After seeing these anomalies at night continually, one of these strange craft flew directly over Tom's home. Then a bigfoot shows up after sending out thoughts. Normal.

Tom watched the sky every night. From his bathroom window, Tom was able to get an amazing view of the surrounding landscape and a grand vantage point to view the lights, drones whatever they were.

He decided to take out the screen of his bathroom window for a clearer view of the field. Then nightfall came. The stars were out and his wife joined him. She was skeptical until she saw something that defies explanation.

They noticed a small cluster of stars that seemed a lot brighter than all the others. His wife noticed that they were seemingly shooting beams of light at one another. These lights were different colors.

His wife called out. "Am I tripping or are those stars sending colored light beams to one another?" They both looked on in awe. Tom confirmed he was seeing the same thing. Then came the light show finale.

As if "they" were putting on a show for them, Tom and his wife weren't sure these were stars. A light suddenly appeared over a distant hill. An enormous orange orb the size of a tractor-trailer emerged into view. It had a fiery-plume exhaust and it screamed across the sky in front of them. It was like they had a front row seat to the event. It was completely silent!

As soon as it appeared it headed towards the tops of the trees and then disappeared. It went out like a flashlight. Tom and his wife were both blown away by this event which happened around 10pm. He called me and I remember looking at the phone, but because I was half-asleep I didn't pick up. I wish I did!

We talked about the event the next morning over the phone. Upon further digging - he revealed from his vantage point during the day that the tractor-trailer sized object did not emerge from behind the hill, it came from the field below! He and his wife had witnessed something taking off from the field, with propulsion and the ability to go invisible by cloaking itself or somehow vanishing by some other means.

I talked with Jon Wilk, one of the Bigfoot researchers that I work with. We discuss various cases and after talking to him about this encounter just outside of Leominster State Forest, he tells me that several years back he was investigating a case in Tom's same neighborhood of a home owner witnessing several sasquatch running through the fields in the middle of the night. They were tall enough that they were bigger than the corn stalks in the corn field. The homeowner has been watching and witnessing this Bigfoot activity for years and was finally coming forward and reported his experiences.

This witness had corroborated Tom's story. Bigfoot sightings in the same area. Visual ones. Tom is still very animated and expressive when he describes his bigfoot encounter today. What he saw was freaky and terrified him. As an avid hunter and outdoorsman, he couldn't believe that something like this was living in the woods...near his home...in Massachusetts.

20

CLOAKING BIGFOOT?

On my podcast *Monsterland*, Matty and I had Jonathan Wilk of Squatchachusetts discuss some of the latest and strangest cases of sasquatch encounters in Massachusetts. There was one in particular that I was hoping he would discuss. His own story is amazing to say the least, but this one involves a researcher who has been making frequent excursions to Leominster State Forest. This researcher, Mike, has paid close attention to the Elm Street entrance of the forest.

Here's a little background on his experience - then I will deliver the whopper.

Mike has been into this section of the forest on several occasions. He noticed something odd. He found small stick structures. These were shaped like little tee-pees or pyramids and used with broken thick branches, not cut by a saw, and they were off trail.

There were about five or six of them. They were about the

right size for a child to put together. He believed that they matched larger structures that he has seen in the western part of the state. Mike was extremely excited to share his experience.

"Ronny, I think there might be a nursery in this section of the forest." I looked at him in disbelief. "The mid-state trail runs through Leominster State Forest and this could be a migratory route and this could possibly be a stop along the way to feed. They could possibly be leaving some of the younger ones at this location to keep them busy, while the adults hunt. These structures could be what they will be building as they grow older" Mike smiled.

"But that's not it. When I was in amongst the structures, I got the sense that I was being watched. Then, a guttural yell like a gorilla began. I was being screamed at!"

Mike's eyes were open wide and he explained that he got the message and took off running.

A year or so has passed since Mike's last incident with being screamed at from what I understand. After spending the day on Elm Street, he was making his way back to the dirt parking lot and was coming to the state forest gate at the entrance. He turned around to look back at the woods. He had come up empty but had the thought to take a look one last time before he climbed into his car.

Mike looks out along the trail and notices a figure. This creature is on two legs standing alongside a tree. He doesn't see a face, but he can see that this thing is hairy, with a black color, and it is about six to seven feet tall.

He can't believe his eyes. He looks deeper down the trail and notices that there is a hiker off in the distance making his way towards the entrance where Mike is positioned. This hiker is far off enough that Mike isn't sure that the hiker can see what Mike is seeing. A bigfoot.

Then the creature and Mike make eye contact. Mike realizes now that the creature was watching the hiker in the distance making his way towards both of them. Mike was initially looking at the back of the sasquatch's head until it turned to look at him.

They lock eyes for a few seconds and the creature casually turns and begins to slowly and calmly walk away. Mike can't believe he is witnessing this. He doesn't want to look away. I am glad that he didn't because what happens next is life changing.

As the sasquatch is walking away, its gait and motion similar to that of the Patterson-Gimlin film, something begins to happen. Graceful and not worried that Mike was going to harm it, it's hand slowly begins to vanish before Mike's eyes.

Like the movie, *Predator,* the creature then began to cloak itself, or go invisible. Whatever you want to call it, the creature turned invisible from the hand, to the arm, then the legs, until it completely disappeared into thin air.

Poof. The bigfoot was now gone.

21
CHANNELING CATHRYN

I met Cathryn, a local published author, at the New England Authors Expo this year. Cathryn McIntyre is the author of *"The Thoreau Whisperer: Channeling the Spirit of Henry David Thoreau"*. At a very young age, seven to be exact, she began to have visitors while growing up in Pontiac, Michigan. There were gray aliens in her closet and blinding light coming into her bedroom window. Her mother would assure her that what she was experiencing were only dreams.

Figments of the imagination? They continued to happen no matter how often she was told they were only dreams. She knew that they were real. Strange bumps would appear behind her ears from time to time. Her mother noticed them when they first emerged. They would disappear as quickly as they came, but Cathryn is confident that she was and is being tracked. These were implants of some kind.

Cathryn began writing very early on and she felt that part of what she was writing was channeled. The information she was writing was being given to her, as if from the ether, the other side. These characters and people she was interacting with while she was writing, she believes to be spirits. One of the spirits she believes she has made contact with is none other than local writer, Henry David Thoreau. She also believes some of these spirit guides are alien.

As with most UFO abductees, Cathryn realized that she had a gift. She was psychic. She could see things before they would happen and she would get information...that well, came from somewhere else and from someone else. She would often know when famous celebrities were about to die days before; she was always picking up information. Some call this God or the universe, or "Spirit". She believes that because she is open to Spirit - these different spirits and the invisible world in which they dwelled were coming forward.

While growing up, around twelve years of age, Cathryn knew and often told her mother that she would be moving to Boston. She moved to Massachusettts in her early twenties. When she moved, the UFO phenomena moved with her. She believes that she has implants that are still tracking her.

Living in Cambridge, she joined MUFON in the early 1990's and met with other experiencers who shared similar frightening instances and encounters with the otherworldly. She wanted to decipher what had happened to her during the 1960's as a child. What was the reality?

She began to meet with other experiencers and a week before one of these group meetings, Cathryn received a phone call. When she picked up the receiver and put it up to her ear, she heard a series of strange beeps and noises. Almost as if it was a programming code giving the implants an update. When she arrived at the UFO meeting a week later, one of the members asked the group if they had received a strange phone call last week.

"Did you all get that tune-up call?" she asked. Six of the

people, about half of the group raised their hands. They confirmed that they had heard those strange sounds as well. Yikes. Who is in control of those implants? What was that phone call about?

In 2007, Cathryn began to meet with another group of experiencers, made up of many members of the Harvard University's Dr John Mack's original UFO support group. It was during one of these meetings with this group that Cathryn wrote about in her book, *The Thoreau Whisperer*, when Thoreau cautioned them not to believe everything they were being told by the aliens.

While she was reading the chapter in *Monsterland* where I was highlighting the UFO flaps and waves that flooded Michigan in 1966 and 1967, it hit her, "Hello, I was there! I was living there during those UFO sightings!" This was the same time that she was starting to have her experiences while at the young age of seven.

One of these experiences Cathryn knew was beyond a doubt real. She wasn't making this stuff up. She could actually see the little grays in her room. There were three of them. She felt herself being beamed out of her bed and floated out of the window. She was then put back into her bed and began to scream for her mother.

Her mother came in and told her to be quiet and go to sleep but she insisted. "Mom, I can see them, there is one in the closet, one in the dining room...". They scattered when her Mom came into the room, but Cathryn could see them hiding with her mind's eye. They were invisible. She didn't realize how or why she was able to do this. She would later learn that despite her Mom's continued efforts to dissuade her from believing in these "dreams", her Mom was psychic as well.

There was another experience in Michigan that Cathryn would never forget. "When I was living in Michigan, around

1979, I was around 20 years old and going to college. I was living off campus in this apartment and had this very clear abduction experience there...and that one involved this orb. A reddish-colored orb. I had forgotten about it and didn't remember it until I read your book!" said Cathryn.

"The experience started where I was in a semi-dreamlike state. It started with seeing someone looking at my car. There was someone, a man looking, bent down at my car. I was like, what, who is that looking at my car? Then I heard this voice that said "Don't worry about your car, look at this. You can either take this path or that path."

The voice showed Cathryn her life. If she chose the first path, a life of material and wealth, it would be great and she would have everything she would want, but she would die in a horrific car crash, Or she can take this other path, the spiritual, and the voice suggested that this other path, the path that she is on now, listening to spirit, is the right path. "This is the path that you should take."

Cathryn was trying desperately to wake up from this "dream". "This reddish-orb thing was in the corner of my bedroom when I woke up." She gets up out of her bed. "Now I can see the orb is in the living room. I walked into the living room and looked out the front window and notice this man on a motorcycle looking at my car. He was bent down, leaning down and looking at my car." It was just like in the beginning of her dream.

Cathryn then heard the same voice, this strong voice, from her dream say "It starts now." She went back to bed and proceeded to have the dream all over again! Did "They" somehow stop time? Do they have the ability to adjust time by realigning people that would help to make a difference in bringing a greater awareness? Is this just a dream?

The evening before Cathryn and I met she wanted to "tune into" sasquatch to learn more about what they are. She was given the image of a hand. A hairy hand that was enormous, but her focus was on the fingertips. Similar to a human hand and the nails were black and resembled claws that would resemble that of a dogs, but the fingernail in the human hand replaced with this dog-like claw.

She got the impression that "the sasquatch" in this area were showing her that they are very similar to humans - but more animal like a bear or dog? The hand was hairless until it got to the wrist. Brownish, black hair protruded from the rest of the arm in the image she received. As we sat at our interview spot near the pond, Cathryn kept glancing towards the hillside and the treeline from where we sat. She was shifting a bit in her seat and you could see that she was starting to pick up on something.

With her arm extended and her finger pointed she created an invisible line going back and forth from the hillside to the pond. "What is over that hillside there? I keep on getting this feeling from here to there". "As if they are coming down from the hillside and using this pond for food?" I asked. "Yes." she replied with a nod. "Are you getting more than one? That there are several sasquatch here in this area?" I asked. Cathryn responded firmly, "Yes there are."

A week later, I would get an email from Cathryn.

Hi Ronny - I woke up today thinking how crazy I am for even thinking that yesterday's incident was Bigfoot related. Then I walked out to my car and stepped on something next to the car in the driveway. A green apple! I look around me - trees all around - none of them apple trees! I look around - no other apples on the ground anywhere - driveway is 5 lanes wide - no other apples! Hope I don't sound entirely nutty but it seems like something is going on here.

I asked her if she requested a "gift" from them.

"I asked for a sign - since I was busy doubting myself (per usual). And I left off another detail - an intensely animal like smell was in the air around the house last night. There are a lot of wild animals in this area so it could have been anything. I don't know what to think. Maybe I'm losing it."

She asked for something and she got it. What's interesting is what it was. An apple. Apples are associated with Leominster, being that it is the birthplace of Johnny Appleseed, I took this as a sign confirming that this was from them.

I have had several people tell me while they were reading or just finished reading my book that they received marbles. One in particular was with my Aunt who pulled into her parking spot at work. When she stepped out of her car she almost stepped on a marble that was just sitting there. She had just started the chapter about marbles in my book. It freaked her out just a bit.

22

THE INVISIBLES

What can the ocean (pun intended!) and dolphins teach us about Sasquatch? Meet Joan Ocean. Joan Ocean is internationally known for her work in the field of human-dolphin and whale communications. She is a psychologist and scientist who co-founded the Dolphin Connection International, which is an organization that explores the advancement of human consciousness, biophysics and spirituality. The organization's main goal of encouraging friendship and communication between people and ocean swimming dolphins and whales.

Joan had an experience with a California Gray Whale, which came very close to the island shores of British Columbia, looking directly into her eyes. She experienced a communication between herself and the whale that changed her life forever. She realized that these beings were trying to communicate with her. How this all started was through meditation. She was beckoned to the water.

While swimming in Hawaii she was approached by a pod of more than a hundred Spinner dolphins. Surrounding her, they continued to swim with her for two miles. She felt that they were communicating with her through her feelings and intuition. She believes that they are multidimensional beings. Through tuning into the vibrational frequencies, she is able to access the same wavelength as the dolphins and whales.

She experiences the communication with these water beings as holographic sound, which is a language that intensifies physical senses, bypasses the rational brain and resonates directly with our cellular intelligence.

After writing several books about her communications with these ocean species, she was asked by someone via email how she communicated. His reasoning? He was looking for a way to communicate with Bigfoot. If it was working with dolphins and whales, why not Sasquatch.

This led to an amazing discovery for Joan. She now believes, through her own personal research and experience, that sasquatch has skills beyond our comprehension. By spending time alone in the woods, for weeks at a time, she was introduced to the so-called myth.

Joan is convinced that Sasquatch knows how to shape-shift. They can de-materialize at will. They can create infrasound that affects the environment, the same way lions, tigers and killer whales have been able to demonstrate. Sasquatch has the ability to travel 300 miles a day on foot and they also live in well-lighted underground facilities, almost like a Bigfoot underground railroad.

Through previous secret interactions with humans from our past, they learned how to read and write. This feat has been claimed by many researchers that have been having direct contact with these people of the forest. Like the Native Americans have mentioned, Sasquatch has been contacting and lives with the Star People.

There have been some stories of missing time when dealing with sasquatch. It seems that Joan Ocean truly believes that they have the capacity and ability to manipulate time somehow. Telepathy, time-manipulation, this all falls in line with something more alien than animal. They supposedly can tell us about our past and our future. Sasquatch has been here on this planet longer than the human race has been in existence.

There is a lot of speculation to there being any sasquatch on the island of Hawaii, but Joan believes there are indeed Bigfoot there. Not knowing that the interactions she was experiencing in the jungle the week she spent alone in her tent was sasquatch, she dismissed them is odd occurrences. On her first night she had rocks thrown at her and her tent they also made strong musty smells that enveloped all around her. One night it was so strong that she was unable to even sleep.

They also created what sounded like trees falling to the ground with loud crashes. When she awoke in the morning, to her surprise, there were no trees on the ground. Sasquatch are able to mimic sounds like birds, high-pitched haunting and spooky. One night, during her solo camping excursion she awoke in her tent with the feeling of someone pushing on her shoulder...but there was nothing there. Just like Les Stroud.

NATIVE AMERICANS AND THE STAR PEOPLE

"Accounts of luminous orbs and beings suddenly appearing out of thin air are not new. There have been many reports of such phenomena during my travels. These incidents are most often described in concert with the appearance of UFOs.

Luminous orbs are very familiar to indigenuous peoples. Accounts of radiant orbs transforming into UFOs have been reported on many occasions. Reports of glowing orbs shapeshifting into star beings are fairly common among American Indian encounters; appearances of the brilliant dancing orbs during ceremonies have also been described. Hope dancers are often visited by shimmering globes.

The Cherokee claim luminous balls have been seen in their homeland since ancient times. The legend has it the lights are the wives and mothers of warriors looking for their loved ones. The Shuar Indians of the Amazon report being visited by their ancestors who appear in the night skies as luminous white or blue spheres. The Shuan do not differentiate among ancestors or UFOs or themselves. They perceive them as the same, all ultimately are us."

Rodrigo an elderly Zapotec Indian told the author of the book *Sky People* about glowing orbs visiting the elders of his tribe. The star people are invisible to most people on earth. They do not see them. People have forgotten to look beyond what the eyes can see. At one time every human had this ability. But they got lazy and lost the power. They are not aware the star people walk among us. They are invisible to their eyes. Lacandon Indians are a tribe that communicate with the invisible.

They still practice the old ceremonies of their ancestors in their villages. There is a ceremony that is performed for all things visible and all things invisible. Sometimes the star people appear at their ceremonies. The author asks how is it that they can show themselves. Many people have seen the balls of light but not all have seen the humanoid appearance of the invisibles. To see the invisible, you have to look inside yourself. The modern day people are ruled by law - not by heart.

CANADIAN COIN REVEALS UFO

The recognition of different countries and their UFO encounters is significant in the "Disclosure" effort. On October 2, 2019, the Canadian government and the Royal Canadian Mint announced that they would be commemorating the Shag Harbour UFO incident with a one-of-a-kind coin. The incident occurred on October 4th, 1967 when a luminous and large UFO, witnessed by fisherman and the townspeople, crashed into the Atlantic Ocean off the coast of Nova Scotia, Canada. This isn't the first time. A year before, the Royal Canadian Mint released a coin commemorating the Falcon Lake UFO Incident.

Residents contacted the Royal Canadian Mounted Police and alerted them that a large and extremely bright object had crashed into the water. It was investigated by RCMP, discovering traces of something strange, a yellow glowing foam at the confirmed crash location. The report filed was that no craft, plane or object was recovered from the scene.

Residents did report however, that a glowing object was seen flying above Shag Harbour and then a "dark object' was observed floating on the surface of the ocean. The Canadian Navy, with ships in close proximity, was asked to send divers to investigate. It is reported that nothing was found. But over the years, rumors will not go away that there was something discovered, recovered and removed from the floor of the ocean.

One of the witnesses to the event, Laurie Wickens, now a 67-year-old former fisherman, called the local RCMP about the incident and explained:

"There were four (lights) in a row, and they were going on and off," says Wickens, at the time a 17-year-old driving home to Shag Harbour with a friend and three young women. "One would come on, then two, three and four -- and they'd all be off for a second and come back on again."

Soon afterwards, Wickens was among a dozen or so people gathered at the water's edge, watching in amazement as a glowing orange sphere -- about the size of a city bus -- bobbed on the waves about 300 metres from the shore. Per witnesses, this craft didn't crash into the water, it intentionally slipped silently under the surface of the water at 11:20 PM.

In the book "*Dark Object: The World's Only Government-Documented UFO Crash*", co-authored by Chris Styles who eventually interviews former military insiders and members of the navy's Fleet Diving Unit, was told there was no crash. The orange orb spotted in Shag Harbour had submerged under its own power and travelled to a spot on the seabed off Shelburne.

As like most locations with an abnormal amount of UFO and orb sightings, this area at the time of this incident was the location of a top-secret *U.S. military base*. It was disguised as an oceanographic institute! The truth would eventually surface in the 1980's about this secret base and that the facility used underwater microphones and magnetic detection devices to track enemy submarines. Were they really tracking submarines or USOs? Was this an orb or a drone of some kind? Was it ours? The Canadians? The aliens?

So what is so special about the coin? The Royal Canadian mint created these square coins with pure silver, depicting four ORANGE LIGHTS hovering in the sky above as three fishermen are watching and pointing! Here's the incredible part, with a black-light flashlight, an enormous and *INVISIBLE* flying saucer-looking craft is revealed and appears on the coin. The orange orbs or lights on the coin are fixtures of the craft. We are only able to see the lights with our normal vision and normal light. We need special lights to see the invisible.

Are the powers that be quietly trying to tell us something?

23

EXETER UFO FESTIVAL

I had the opportunity and pleasure to speak this year at *The Exeter UFO Festival* in Exeter, New Hampshire. The entire town gets involved and it was a full house when I did my presentation. My daughter Aysia joined me and ran my table, helping me sell my books. Based on a conversation with my wife Amy the night before, I decided to change up my presentation and talk about some of the stranger aspects of Sasquatch as well as synchronicity. I was using more of my personality and cracking jokes, and the crowd was super engaged.

I discussed my experiences with receiving marbles which I detail in my first book. The idea of gifting and receiving gifts from sasquatch. I figure the only way we are going to understand this phenomenon, is by collaborating and sharing our stories. We were all here for a reason in this Exeter Town Hall right now.

"We all have had an experience or we are so curious and intrigued by this subject matter, there is more going on than we think." After my presentation people began to raise their hands, sharing their strange encounters that they couldn't understand. It became a support group for a short period of time where attendees were confessing to things they hadn't shared with others before. It was amazing, and I too admit, it takes a lot of courage to do that.

I got off the stage after my presentation, and I was cornered almost immediately by ten people with books in their hands for me to sign. It was astonishing to me the amount of personal stories and experiences that are out there in the world. After I signed the last book, I grabbed my laptop from the stage and headed for the exit as they prepared for the next speaker. With my laptop under my arm, I made my way to the double doors exiting Exeter Town Hall and to the table set ups.

When I opened the doors, I literally walked right into my friend Phil. Strangely, at that exact moment, a single white marble dropped to the floor. It bounced off the marble floor loudly and rolled. I stood in shock. "Where did that come from?" Phil bends down and picks up the marble handing it to me. "You dropped your marble brother."

"That's not mine. That's not your marble?" I asked. Phil shook his head. "Nope". "What the hell, that came out of nowhere!" The white marble just appeared. It materialized and seemed to come right out of my laptop, which is impossible! I looked at Phil sideways, thinking to myself, "Is he messing with me?" He wasn't the type to do this. I shrugged it off and we said our hello's.

Minutes later, I walked into the room where the speakers had their tables set up. There was a small crowd around my table and Aysia looked up at me smiling. I looked down at the table and I was shocked to see six marbles lined up on the table next to one another! "Where did those marbles come from!?"

"I don't know. They were in the bottom of my bag. Noah must have put them there."

No way. This couldn't be. What a strange coincidence?

HELL'S HIGHWAY

My daughter Aysia and I decided to take on a three-hour hike into Leominster State Forest. Entering Elm Street, we walked along the Parmenter Road path, which leads to the Hell's Highway Trail.

As an experiment, before I left the house, I proclaimed out loud that I would love to receive a crow's feather along my hike. The reasoning was that crows are thought to have a part in Sasquatch activity. The sasquatch reportedly are able to use the crows as some kind of spiritual drone. Sasquatch has the ability to access the spirit of the crow, using their eyes to see. I also requested a white stone. Something shiny, like a white quartz, that is also supposed to have some significance. Items like these are often gifted back and used as a gift to sasquatch. The idea was that I would hope we would find these specific items on our hike. If we were to receive these items, it would be beyond coincidental.

As we were walking through the middle of the hike, I also requested to see an orb. "It would be great to see a little white orb dancing around in the forest in front of us while we are here". Keeping my eyes peeled the entire way, we came to the end of the hike empty handed. "Well, that's disappointing. We didn't get the black crow feather, the white stone or get to see a white orb." We headed home, sweating and in need of sustenance.

My second oldest daughter, Lena, came home from school that day. She went downstairs to retrieve something and then came bolting back upstairs. Frantically, she says she saw a small white orb fly by her face. Her timing was curious. The next day my daughter Aysia is back at school. Along the path she is running on for gym class, she spies a black crow feather along her run path. Looking down, she notices and marvels that she seemingly has received a crow's feather, as I requested - just not on the hike as we had wished.

Ironically, that same day, on her way home after school, Aysia spots something shiny and white in the asphalt sidewalk in front of her. As she gets closer, as if placed appropriately in a small crack directly in Aysia's path, a white marble with three stripes, one green, one orange and one blue, glistens in the sun.

She bends down and picks it up. Her heart skips a beat. She walks in the door after school and tells me about the feather and the marble. I am amazed at the fact that we received all three items as requested within a twenty-four hour period. They showed up in Aysia's and Lena's path the next day.

Just a few days later, Aysia would find a conspicuously placed rock in her path again. This stone was found in her estimation about ten feet away from the spot where she discovered the marble a few days before. She came running home to show me this strange stone. It's wild but - the stone is a Shamanic stone. After Aysia identified the stone, which I confirmed looked exactly like pictures we had discovered. Bubbly metal balls, almost looking...like orbs...or marbles protruding from the surface of the stone. I researched the metaphysical properties of the find. Was this from someone's rock collection?

It doesn't seem like the stone is from around here. After some research, we learned it is commonly found in marine deposits in Australia, Russia, India, Brazil, China, South

Africa and Gabon. I scratched my head as I started reading more about it.

"A shamanic stone, Pyrolusite provides protection from the intentions of those who populate the lower frequencies of the Astral World and during ritual work. Pyrolusite is known as the stone of transformation, use to undue mental influences. Known to be an excellent grounding crystal for meditation and healing it is ideal for body layouts. It is also said to enhance the linear flow of energies equally.

Ancient magicians relied upon this bleak, dark gray colored stone, known as Pyrolusite because of its power to transform and restructure energies. It is an extremely useful stone to sustain close to an individual and to place in his immediate surroundings. With an eventual ability to tone up the aura and helps one to feel more optimistic about life.

By activating the base chakra, it repels negative energy and lays the foundation of physical vitality and spiritual energy for the wearer's torso. It encourages serendipity to come into play and holds stronger effect on the crown chakra which aids transformation.

The most common manganese mineral, Pyrolusite protects the wearing individual from earth demons as they throw off their spells. Today this rock is still worshipped as a premier talisman of fortification, an intuitive protective shield deflecting and dispelling negative energies, or disparaging forces. It serves the wearer to see the love of the universe and also keeps a spiritual awareness. It drives off the evil, negative powers and dispels all the psychic attacks.

Excellent at repelling negativity, it is a powerful grounding stone which is electrical in nature...it provides a link between Earth and the human heart."

"The Shamans say that the reason we take on a physical body is to evolve and grow, to acquire emotional maturity and wisdom. To use a metaphor from physics, when we're embodied, we're like an electron in a particle state, while in the invisible world, we're like an electron in a wave state. The particle state is our "local" nature - flesh and blood, sitting on a couch reading. The wave state is our "nonlocal" nature, in which we extend to the farthest reaches of the universe, at one with all things. When we did and leave this body behind, we return to our nonlocal nature, to the formless invisible world. But the shamans of old learned to experience their nonlocal selves without dying - to taste One Spirit while still in the everyday world."

Dr. Alberto Villoldo (One Spirit Medicine)

In April of 2016, researchers from Northwestern University published in the journal Scientific Reports, that when human sperm meets an egg, it sets of a spark of light that can last up to two hours! This light is invisible to the naked eye and must be viewed microscopically.

The same idea is referenced by famed author Carlos Castaneda, that people in essence are like an egg of energy. We are spiritual beings of light having a human experience or existence. We start off as a spark of light upon conception of life between the sperm and the egg. We go through life with this growing egg of energy, this aura or our true essence.

This energy field interacts with all the others and can transcend space and time. When we die, we have heard that we head down this dark tunnel and see the "light" at the other end. Is it possible that we return back to this source becoming light once again? When we leave this physical form, I wonder if we ourselves, turn into balls of light and these orbs that people have recorded and photographed.

The shaman is a universal figure found throughout a lot of different cultures around the world. The word shaman means "The one who sees in the dark", but how shamans truly "see" is through their heart. Shamans realize that they are one with nature and they, we for that matter, are in reality connected with everything.

Dr. Alberto Villoldo's highlights in his book *Shaman, Healer, Sage* that the shaman is able to see the invisible worlds that intersect with our own, "For the shaman there is no supernatural heaven. Only the natural world exists, with its visible and invisible realms, among them the spirit world."

Spirit is a vast and invisible energy field that we join with to dream the world into being. It is not a deity with a human within...Spirit is the creative matrix that keeps life in the cosmos evolving and renewing itself."

"The veil that stands between us and the invisible matrix is only a trick of consciousness created by our beliefs. It is said that we have to "see it to believe it," but the converse is actually true: we have to believe it to see it. Otherwise, we don't grasp what's right in front of us because our mind dismisses the information. Research shows that our mental biases are so strong that we easily dismiss sensory information that doesn't fit with our preconceived notions of reality.

Reality and belief is necessary in order for shamans and everyday people like you and I, to manipulate energy and manifest certain outcomes or situations through the universe by the way of the "Law of Attraction". We all do this knowingly or unknowingly with our own energy in the form of thoughts, words and actions. Our thoughts deliver particular outcomes that we blindly believe are not connected to how we see the world. Buddha said, "What we think we become". Our thoughts become our reality. Thoughts, which are the mind's energy, can directly influence the body's physical makeup.

In the book *Animal Speak*, the author highlights that these other realms and the beings that inhabit them are here to help us. Our cultural backgrounds and religions dictate in what form they appear to us.

"The reality of spirit beings and their assistance to those in the physical has been a part of every major religion. The Greeks spoke to the spirits and gods through oracles. The Bushmen of Africa developed ritual and myth from the movements and activities of animals such as the eland and mantis. The Native Americans imitated animals in dance and ritual to establish links to the spirit realm. Belief in the most spiritual realms of life and all its varied manifestations is universal. The most common belief in many societies is that spiritual guides often use animals or animal imagery to communicate their purpose and roles to humans. They could come in the form of saints, angels, ancestral contact, fairies and elves, demons, and even animal totems. Most ancient societies studied the natural world in order to understand the supernatural."

This invisible realm does indeed exist and cultures have known about it for a very long time. With greater awareness, answers to who we are; where we are going, and most importantly why we are here, are within arms (or minds!) reach.

"The awareness that we exist in both the visible and the invisible worlds at the same time brings the realization that everything in your life is something that you have dreamed into being from the invisible matrix of energy. This invisible matrix of wisdom where everything is intertwined, where

every thought we have impacts every cell in our body and every molecule in the cosmos. Quantum physics offers us another apt metaphor in the phenomenon known as entanglement: particles are mysteriously interlinked in such a way that even if they are at opposite ends of the galaxy, if you change the direction in which one particle is spinning, the other immediately reverses its spin. At first scientists thought entanglement might be a demonstration of faster-than-thought communication. Later they understood that it was simply the nature of related particles."

Everything is energy. All energy has consciousness, even the most basic and primitive. An intrusive energy, like a spirit, can have an almost human-like appearance. Quantum perspective reveals that the universe is an integration of interdependent energy fields that are entangled in a meshwork of interactions.

"Quantum physics discovered that physical atoms are made up of vortices of energy that are constantly spinning and vibrating; each atom is like a wobby spinning top that radiates energy. Because each atom has its own specific energy signature (wobble), assemblies of atoms (molecules) collectively radiate their own identifying energy patterns. So every material structure in the universe, including you and me, radiates a unique energy signature."

24

A NEW ADVENTURE

With the goal of trying to make a solid second season of the Monsterland Podcast, we decided to focus on not having a visual recording element to the podcast, to avoid scheduling conflicts. We would strictly push the podcast into the radio show / hybrid podcast world. POD617 was behind us and we were full steam ahead.

Through our friend and producer Kerri, Matty and I met with television producer Seanbaker Carter. We hit it off. We developed a TV show with Seanbaker and his team at Magilla Entertainment / MixTape Entertainment and planned to pitch it to History and Travel Channel networks to start.

Matty wrote a sample script and overall concept for Monsterland as a stand-alone television show showcasing Matty and I investigating recent sightings and encounters. A show where we would go to various hotspots around Monsterland and New England that we could investigate as the activity was happening.

I created a game plan and wrote out summaries for thirteen episodes for Season one. I researched and compiled another fifty ideal locations for future seasons. The goal with the Monsterland television show was this - we wanted to show the connection between all of this phenomena. But could we prove it? Heck, that's what my first book *Monsterland* is all about...that there is this connection between all of this phenomena.

After about six months of developing, writing, and meetings, we had something presentable. Meetings were set up and had the show "Monsterland" pushed into the pre-green light meetings for both Travel and History channel. We thought for sure that this was it. My wife Amy was confident. "Babe, you are going to sell the show. It may not be this time or this show, but it is coming. I can feel it."

This was going to happen. I could feel it too. Matty had a dream of a film crew driving down a dirt road. We were in the middle of nowhere and we were looking for bigfoot. He also recalls that there were some members of the film crew that were musicians and we stopped at a local bar where they were jamming out with the locals. All signs pointed to this was about to pop. Unfortunately, our show concept didn't make it past either of those green light meetings. We were humbly crushed.

I truly felt that we would be seeing Monsterland, the book, the podcast, the place with so many encounters finally become a television show. It wasn't meant to be. At least not in that form at that time.

Fast forward a few months and I am leaving for the Pacific Northwest in less than forty-eight hours to look for Bigfoot. I am traveling to the other side of the country for almost a month to film a television show with people I don't even know.

My wife Amy looks at me, "You have to do this. You are meant to do this. This was meant to happen! You better enjoy every second of this or I am going to be pissed at you!"

As long as I had her blessing, I was on my way. This just doesn't happen to everyone. I didn't seek this out. It found me. I am supposed to do this. I know that all the previous events in my life have led me to this very point.

Could this be it? Could we find evidence of this mysterious man of the woods? Would we actually find Bigfoot or evidence that leads to the discovery of this creature - one of the Universe's mysteries?

I am leaving my family, my wife and four kids to take on this crazy adventure. I am going to be living in a tent and in hostile territory littered with mountain lions and black bears. Night investigations and smack dab in a sasquatch hot spot right during the middle of calving season.

I am heading on a scientific expedition in the search for Sasquatch. It's being filmed for The Travel Channel. Holy shit.

25
MAY THE SOURCE
BE WITH YOU

"In the universe there is an immeasurable, indescribable force which shamans call intent, and absolutely everything that exists in the entire cosmos is attached to intent by a connecting link."

— **Carlos Castaneda**

"Somehow, our consciousness is the reason the universe is here."

— **Roger Primrose**

(Mathematical Physicist / Philosopher of Science)

With the realization and confirmation that UFOs are real and that they do indeed exist, the concept of reality becomes the bigger question. What else exists that we have long believed to be part of our imagination? We don't know who or what is behind the wheel of these craft. What if some of these ships are not piloted but are alive and conscious within themselves?

I am sure we will at some point find out who "they" are. They could be a long-lost civilization, an alien race from another dimension or even ourselves from the future.

There is a reason that this "truth" has been reserved for only a select few. The winds have shifted however, and we are beginning to see what lies behind the veil. Some of us may not be ready to see this truth, or to hear it, but like UFOs, we may learn about "hidden beings" like sasquatch that have been stuck in the world of fable and myth.

Through my research, I have come to the conclusion that there seems to be a strong connection between consciousness, shamanism, UFOs and even Sasquatch. In Shamanism everything is alive and has a spirit. It is an animist tradition, which believes that everything has a spiritual access to it, typically described as being a soul.

As I described in Monsterland, I truly believe that human beings were capable of doing things that we would now deem paranormal, psychic or strange, but on a larger scale. These abilities include communicating with realms within nature, visiting the dreamworld and other places through some form of astral projection or altered state. Things that might otherwise be labeled as simply our imagination gone wild. Many of us no longer remember how to communicate with plants, trees, rocks or weather spirits, but some of our ancestors did. They realized that everything is connected and everything is energy.

In our not so distant past, the path of the shaman was used by hunters and gatherers who had the responsibility of finding food for the tribe. They did this by connecting to the spirits of nature. By accessing expanded states of consciousness or awareness they gained access to this invisible world, in essence, asking for permission to locate the game or other sustenance that lay waiting in the forest.

The Druids believed that the gateway to other realms was hidden in many aspects through nature, including even our own bodies serving as portals. This ability allowed them to influence or manipulate nature or even the weather. You may have heard of the term Native American "rain dances" where members of a tribe would dance with the intention of bringing much needed rainwater to their lands in order to survive.

The concept of God was discovered to be not an entity with a beard, but the force that connects everything and can be found in everything. Nature itself, the universe, is indeed alive. It is conscious. The shamans, as well as the druids, were masters when it came to working with nature. They knew that through this alignment with nature, a force would activate and open these deeply hidden psychic abilities inherent in all of us. They mastered the ability to experience a connection with the worlds that are within reach to all of us, but remain invisible to most.

We all experience a hint of this connection through different experiences in nature. The best way I could describe this connection with nature would be when I was a young child. I remember having this ingrained belief that I could somehow communicate with animals. There was a connection. I remember being so captivated and taken aback when I would witness a deer or coyote in the wild.

The shamans would, by the use of intent, disassociate their

own consciousness or awareness from their physical body, entering into other realities. This is the world of "things hidden", the shaman's world. The dream world is another place, another level of consciousness, that the indignenous peoples referred to as the spirit world. Shamans believe that the spirit world and the dream world are one in the same.

Throughout many indigenous cultures, the dream world is the real world and this one, our current place we know of as reality - is the dream. For twenty-four hours a day, we are dreaming and the real world has come into existence or being in response to the dreams, not the other way around. As above, so below.

Many also believed that the dream world is being controlled. It has a mind of its own. It is consciousness itself, alive and it is what holds everything together. What we know as God.

Dr. Wayne Dyer is an inspiration to many people all over the world. In his book *The Power of Intention,* he points out something very significant while reading one of Carlos Castaneda's books in which Carlos described the idea of intent as a force that exists in the universe. Dr. Dyer likes to use the term "Source" when defining the Universe. Coincidentally, this is where the word "Sorcerer" is derived from. The sorcerer taps into the source.

The shamans, or the ones that live of the source, learn how to harness this energy. This energy or force is something that the shamans have been able to manipulate. Using their intent coupled with a strong will to see the dream realized into a state of attainment. Thus, making intent or their dreams materialize and become a reality.

Dr. Dyer had an epiphany when he read these two lines in

the book *"The Active Side of Infinity"* by Castaneda:

"Intent is a force that exists in the universe. When sorcerers (those who live of the Source), beckon intent, it comes to them and sets up the path for attainment, which means that sorcerers always accomplish what they set out to do."

What he realized was that intent or intention was not something that one would do, but that it is a force that exists in the universe as an *invisible field of energy*, like gravity. Or is gravity really intention, this invisible force? I wondered if intent and space travel could be connected then I stumbled upon this in my research.

On the website for NASA's "StarChild", an educational website for the Goddard Space Flight Center with content focused on kids interested in the wonders of space and science, (Yes, the National Aeronautics and Space Administration has a website for kids and it is called StarChild, which seems to have a strange eerie significance, they provided an interesting answer for this question "What is gravity?" They answer the question...well sort of.

> *"We don't really know what gravity is. We can define what it is as a field of influence, because we know how it operates in the universe. And some scientists think that it is made up of particles called gravitons which travel at the speed of light. However, if we are to be honest, we do not know what gravity "is" in any fundamental way - we only know how it behaves.*
>
> *Gravity is a force of attraction that exists between any two masses, any two bodies, any two particles. It is not just the attraction between objects and the Earth...It is an attraction that exists between all objects, everywhere in the universe."*

The effect of gravity extends from each object out into space in all directions for an infinite distance. This web of invisible energy is connecting and holding all of us together, everything in the universe together, for that matter.

"Matter can simultaneously be defined as a solid (particle) and an immaterial force field (wave). The fact that matter and energy are one in the same is precisely what Einstein recognized when he concluded that E=mc2. This equation reveals that energy (E) = matter (m, mass) multiplied by the speed of light squared (c2). The universe is one indivisible, dynamic whole in which energy and matter are so deeply entangled it is impossible to consider them as independent elements."

In July of 2017, Chinese scientists successfully teleported a photon into space for the first time. A photon is the basic unit of nature that makes up all light. It is a bundle of electromagnetic energy and is known as an elementary particle.

The scientists were able to accomplish this great feat of teleportation through the effects of quantum entanglement. What Einstein terms "spooky action at a distance".

Instead of physically sending an object through space to reach its destination, they selected another point in space and transferred the information to that point, replicating that photon at its new location. "Beam me up Scotty" science-fiction stuff. Quantum entanglement is not limited by distances. Everything is connected. So that means two particles can interact despite their locations.

We are at the early stages of this when it comes to teleportation of larger objects, but the implications are immense. This could be how UFOs, Sasquatch and other beings from other realms are able to traverse long distances, disappear or reappear at will. They have learned how to harness this energy, this consciousness of the universe.

There are neuroscientists and prominent physicists who are leaning towards the idea of panpsychism, which is the idea that the entire universe is consciousness. Not only does this fall in line with Shamanism, but with Hindu and Buddhist beliefs as well. One of the greatest mysteries of our time is dark matter, which makes up 95% of our universe.

We know that it exists due to the gravitational forces, but much like gravity, we don't know what dark matter really is. The Shaman and the panpsychist both see that the mind is everywhere. It isn't encased in our skulls as we have been taught, but it exists around us like an energy field that connects with all other points in the universe.

Like in Shamanism, panpsychism looks at the idea that a table for example is a collection of particles that each have their own consciousness. So with that, any collection of these particles could be conscious.

With this theory, inanimate objects like rocks, marbles, crystals would be conscious as well as spoons. This is the way that people are able to bend spoons. Like in the movie the Matrix, "Be the Spoon". So even a collection of these particles on a massive scale could be conscious. The earth, what is known as Gaia to the Greeks would indeed be conscious. This ancient idea changes reality. Maybe we are finally waking up and getting back to the source.

There is a very famous rumor of a conversation between Jan Harzan President of MUFON (Mutual UFO Network) and

Ben Rich of Skunkworks. Skunkworks is a division of Lockheed Martin Corporation. It has created super-secret spy planes like the SR-71 Blackbird and others which were apparently housed at Area 51 in Nevada, the worst-kept secret US military base in history. Steve Justice, a former Skunkworks veteran of 30 years is now the Chief Operations Officer for Tom Delonge's *To The Stars Academy*.

The discussion was after a lecture given by Ben at UCLA. Jan Harzan and Ben Rich were discussing the idea of how interstellar propulsion works. Basically UFO propulsion. Ben proclaimed during this conversation back in 1993 that we have learned how to travel to the stars and they found an error in the equations and it won't take a lifetime to do it. Jan ,intrigued with this comment, kept asking Ben more questions pertaining to this propulsion system. Jan wasn't letting up with his inquiries to learn more.

Ben finally turned to Jan and asked "How does ESP work?" "I don't know" replied Harzan. "All points in space and time are connected?" Ben Rich responded. *"That's how it works."*

I wanted to write this book to show that sometimes the paths we take are not the ones that we had intended to take, but there is a reason why you are where you are right now. What you seek could be right around the corner. Once discovered, this path or goal may not look exactly like what you had wanted it to, but it is more than you could have imagined.

There are special ingredients that are needed in order for this path to come together. You must have a passion, a love and energy for what you do. You need to believe in what you are doing no matter what others say or think. Intention is inherent in all things. A tiny seed has intention built inside of it. It is programmed to become what it is meant to be, an oak tree. Right now it is just a seed but in time it will grow and become what it is meant to be. Intention is this creative force, this conscious force that holds this universe together. It is the spark that ignites. It leads us to create our own reality, fulfill our purpose and create our own universe.

We must be in harmony with this force because we are all already connected. It all starts with a dream, which becomes a thought. What we think we become. Imagination, is truly more important than knowledge. Our attention, otherwise known as our energy, can be intended or focused in such a way, that if we are in harmony with the source or the universe, then our path will become clear. Doors will open. Things will happen and you will see the magic that is life. You will see the light. The universe works in such a way that what you put out there you get back. Karma, Love, Intention, these are all forces which connect us all together.

God, the Universe, the Source, lets us know if we are on the right path or not. There are messages being sent. The signs are everywhere, if we choose to pay attention. The people that you meet in your life are not by chance. It is not random. There are no coincidences. Everything happens for a reason.

I was hesitant to continue forward on this path. I have learned that the universe has a way of showing you what your path is. If you are yourself, if you are who you are supposed to be, when you find your purpose, things will happen. If you are looking to FIND your purpose, things will happen. If you are looking for the path, the path will find you.

There were many times that I wanted to give up on my

journey. A lot of times, I wasn't even sure where I was headed. What was my original destination? I think in the end we are all trying to really find ourselves. We are trying to find our purpose and place in this world.

I started off looking to be behind the camera, writing or producing. Now I am in front of the camera, starring in a Travel Channel television series about Bigfoot. For now, this is where I am supposed to be.

We have dreams and desires to be somewhere else, or to be like someone else, but ultimately to be ourselves as God intended. We all have the capacity to make those dreams a reality. We can all make the invisible...visible.

"Imagination is more Important than knowledge."

. **Albert Einstein**

EPILOGUE
MONSTERLANDS ARE EVERYWHERE

Based on my research over the years, I laid out our best chances for locations to film and investigate throughout the United States and put together different and recent sightings in the same area that pertained to UFOs, Bigfoot type creatures and strange balls of light wrapped up with some high strangeness. These are just a few to check out and research for yourself. You just might have one in your own backyard and don't even realize it!

1. ECETI Ranch, Washington

At the foot of Mt. Adams sits ECETI ranch where there have been thousands of eyewitnesses, including prominent scientists and physicists, to the strange phenomena here. Review amazing footage by Rob Freeman of strange lights leaving Mt. Adams. One must visit the west side of the mountain, one of the foremost bigfoot research areas in the world after reports of a disappearing bigfoot leaves tracks at the ranch. Photographs, one in particular is a close up image of an alien taken by Peter Maxwell Slattery. Like

Monsterland, ECETI has a long history of UFO sightings going back hundreds of years according to Native American lore. Some believe that the ranch sits on a stargate.

2. Prairie Creek Reservoir, Illinois

Prairie Creek Reservoir in Illinois is the center of a recent string of winged humanoid sightings. An entire family while boating witnesses a 5-6 foot black mothman-type creature with yellow glowing eyes. A witness comes forward having multiple encounters with silent anomalous orange balls of light. These UFOs have been sighted in this same area for years. Rumors abound that these strange sightings align themselves with a 2,000 year old, oval-shaped Native American burial plot which covers an acre of land.

3. Skinwalker Ranch, Utah

Skinwalker Ranch in Utah is a property that is allegedly the site of paranormal and UFO-related activities. It's name is taken from the skinwalker of Navajo legend concerning malevolent witches. There are unexplained cattle mutilations, sightings of UFOs, black helicopters, dog men and bigfoot.

Of the hundreds of people that have visited the ranch, a large majority have reported that the phenomena has followed them home. Purchased by billionaire Robert Bigelow the ranch has been a live paranormal lab financed in part by the DOD. It is widely believed among researchers that a portal or vortex is above or on the ranch.

4. Joshua Tree, California

Residents have experienced UFOs, bigfoot, missing people and mysterious happenings in Joshua Tree, California. This is the location of the widely popular Contact in the Desert conference. Interesting recent UFO video footage has been taken in recent years, including one from April 2018.

They have the Legend of the Yucca man - a spectral creature that has been reported recently by campers and hikers analyzing a photo still making the rounds from 1990s.

The local Native American elders have a name for the sasquatch in the area. They call these, footprint leaving, supernatural entities "Hairy Devils". Recently a witness comes forward with his encounter of a green fireball - what many natives believe it to be a manifestation of the Takwis or Hairy Devils.

There have also been strange reports emanating close by from Edwards Air Force base. Reports of a creature with large blue eyes and a bigfoot walking onto the base for several days - all were told by their superiors not to engage but to just...observe.

5.   Bridgewater Triangle - Massachusetts

There is a 200 square mile area within southeastern Massachusetts dubbed the Bridgewater Triangle, a hotbed of paranormal activity for centuries. Believed to be cursed by the Native Americans after hundreds were decimated by the colonists, the center of the triangle, the Hockomock swamp has orange orb sightings, bigfoot creatures, giant thunderbirds often resembling pterodactyls and black unmarked helicopters.

Rumors of cult sacrifices and a UFO sighting that predates flight in 1760, this Triangle resembles Monsterland - almost a carbon copy of it and it is less than 40 miles away from Leominster, Massachusetts.

6. Dulce, New Mexico

On the Jicarilla Apache reservation in Dulce, New Mexico, residents claim that the along the mountainside of the Archuleta Mesa, UFOs are seen entering the Dulce Base. Many residents and researchers believe that there is indeed an alien base here.

Not far away, more than 50 years ago, a flying saucer is believed to crash in Roswell, New Mexico. Claims from a former worker that the base is working on mind control and genetic manipulation. A local resident had a recent Bigfoot sighting. Is this an underground secret military base...the base...it is reported to be the hub of a network of underground bases.

7. Catskills, New York

For hundreds of years, medicine men have warned the curious to stay out of the Catskills at night because it is home to many earth spirits that can take the form of man or beast - what we know as shapeshifters.

The Hudson Valley is a well-known hotspot for triangle-shaped UFOs, saucers and orbs for decades. There are a plethora of recent UFO sightings. There is a fresh report from a young man in Rhinebank who had two bigfoot experiences. He found strange tracks around his property and several nights later - heard something bipedal walking on his porch. This unwanted presence was accompanied by banging sounds against the siding of the house.

8.   Big Thicket, Texas

Located in the Piney Woods area of east Texas, the Big Thicket is an 83,000 acre area of vast woodlands. Bragg Road or as the locals call it "Ghost Light Road" seems to be the center of paranormal activity.

From orange orbs, to bigfoot to UFOs, it looks like Texas has its own Monsterland and its massive! The activity has been going on for at least three centuries. Not only have bigfoots been reported - there are sightings of cats the size of African lions - but the color black, like black panthers! A recent case surfaced where a bigfoot was seen with a companion - a black big cat. Most of the sightings of these creatures ended with them vanishing before the witnesses eyes!

9.   The Oregon Vortex, Oregon

Dr. Matthew Johnson, a clinical psychologist, shook the sasquatch world a few years back with his amazing claims of witnessing a bigfoot exiting a portal with two other witness seeing something else - strange creatures. This flesh and blood believer has now changed his tune. The Oregon Vortex seems to be the key to getting the portal to open.

Researchers who have come to investigate the area have reported seeing short, red-eyed creatures which came at the researchers charging but disappeared upon the beam of their flashlight. It is believed that these creatures are there to guard either side of the entrance to the portal.

10. Point Pleasant, West Virginia

Point Pleasant is ground zero for Mothman. Like many locations that have strangeness there is a great calamity or loss of life. On December 15, 1967, 46 people lost their lives when the Silver Bridge collapsed, the Mothman serving as an omen.

Herald-Dispatch columnist Dave Peyton states that the Men in Black made an appearance during this time period as well as recently.

11. Fayette County, Pennsylvania

Seasoned researcher Stan Gordon, author of *Silent Invasion*, has been documenting and investigating the area's strangeness in Pennsylvania since 1959. There is a lot of activity within the area of Fayette County where residents have been seeing bigfoot, ufos and other strange cryptids for decades.

Recent bigfoot tracks have been found at Chestnut Ridge. There was a report describing a glowing orange cylindrical-shaped object in a vertical position hovering only about 80 feet above the ground. Resident Grant Lawrence has had a thunderbird sighting and his encounter actually corroborates similar accounts which describe the creature standing eight feet tall with a wingspan of 15 to 20 feet.

12. Sedona, Arizona

The high desert of Sedona is a place well-known for the

various portals and vortices not to mention the countless accounts of orbs and bigfoot. It also has its own paranormal ranch like that of ECETI and Skinwalker, the Bradshaw ranch which was rumored to be confiscated by the US Government because it sits on one of the biggest interdimensional portals on the planet.

Like Monsterland, you cannot be in the forest at night in the Sedona National park. And yes, the Native Americans believed this area to be sacred just like that of areas in and around Monsterland aka Leominster State Forest.

NOTES

Chapter 2 (The Shaman's Secret)

Villoldo, Dr. Alberto, *Shaman, Healer, Sage,* New York, Penguin, Random House Publishing, 2000

Villoldo, Dr. Alberto, PH.D, *One Spirit Medicine: Ultimate Ways to Ultimate Wellness*, Carlsbad, California, Hay House Publishing, 2015

Chapter 4 (Is it just a Legend?)

Tata, John, *The Boy from Plastic City*, Magnolia, Massachusetts, Fellow Pilgrim Books, 2016

Chapter 6 (What's in the Water?)

https://www.independent.co.uk/news/science/octopus-aliens-scientists-theory-meteors-space-earth-cambrian-aexplosion-a8358631.html

https://www.nbcnews.com/mach/science/oumuamua-object-likely-came-solar-system-very-different-ours-ncna858226

https://www.nytimes.com/2017/12/18/insider/secret-pentagon-ufo-program.html

https://www.thedrive.com/the-war-zone/28305/carrier-group-in-recent-ufo-encounters-had-new-air-defense-tech-just-like-nimitz-in-2004-incident

https://deadline.com/2019/07/area-51-facebook-matty-roberts-interview-1202648871/

http://www.fox10phoenix.com/news/us-world-news/this-is-a-misguided-idea-ufo-whistleblower-bob-lazar-warns-people-not-to-storm-area-51?fbclid=IwAR09sf3BMT0SVesPK4t_Y9Qcl_hKVSXqjlZYV6pys9SqiwBwjBIT4rea4Sw

Tompkins, William Mills, *Selected by Extraterrestrials*, South Carolina, Createspace 2010

Chapter 7 (Monsterland Expands)

Need - Add Spaced Out Radio episode link with Matty and I

Chapter 8 (More Visitors)

UFO Sightings in Massachusetts
http://nuforc.org/webreports/ndxlMa.html

Chapter 9 (Orange You Glad You Can See Me)

http://nuforc.org/webreports/ndxlMa.html

Chapter 14 (Navy and Nordics)

https://www.youtube.com/watch?v=SIOjlLe0l7w

https://ufoholic.com/alien-events/brazilian-psychics-prediction-contact-with-aliens-will-happen-july-2019/

Chapter 16 (The White Wolf)

https://trustedpsychicmediums.com/spirit-animals/praying-mantis-spirit-animal/

https://thriveonnews.com/animal-spirit-praying-mantis/

Chapter 17 (Protectors of the Portals)

https://www.oregonlive.com/trending/2019/07/iconic-author-peter-matthiessen-revealed-as-bigfoot-devotee-claimed-he-spotted-sasquatch-in-northwest.html

https://abcnews.go.com/International/indian-army-tweets-photo-yeti-footprints-deep-himalayas/story?id=62721865

Chapter 18 (Supernatural Sasquatch)

http://www.surajamrita.com/bon/Shambala.html

Moskowitz, Kathy Strain, *Giants, Cannibals & Monsters: Bigfoot in Native Culture,* British Columbia, Hancock House Publishers, 2008

Chapter 19 (Bigfoot Gets Visual)

http://www.lesstroud.ca/survivorman-bigfoot/

http://nuforc.org/webreports/ndxlMa.html

Chapter 21 (Channeling Cathryn)

McIntyre, Cathryn, *The Thoreau Whisperer: Channeling the Spirit of Henry David Thoreau*, Amazon Digital Services, 2018

Chapter 22 (The Invisibles)

http://www.joanocean.com/

Clarke, Ardy Sixkiller, *Sky People: Untold Stories of Alien Encounters in Mesoamerica*, Newburyport, Massachusetts, Red Wheel, Weiser, 2014

https://www.bbc.com/news/world-us-canada-49901449

https://atlantic.ctvnews.ca/canada-s-best-documented-ufo-sighting-still-intrigues-50-years-on-1.3600020

Chapter 23 (Exeter UFO Festival)

https://www.gemexi.com/gemstones/pyrolusite

Chapter 24 (A New Adventure)

Villoldo, Dr. Alberto, *Shaman, Healer, Sage,* New York, Penguin, Random House Publishing, 2000

https://www.sciencealert.com/scientists-just-captured-the-actual-flash-of-light-that-sparks-when-sperm-meets-an-egg

Villoldo, Dr. Alberto, *Shaman, Healer, Sage,* New York, Penguin, Random House Publishing, 2000

Andrews, Ted, *Animal - Speak: The Spiritual & Magical Powers of Creatures Great & Small*, St. Paul, Minnesota, Llewellyn Publications, 2001

Lipton, Bruce, *The Biology of Belief: Unleashing the Power of Consciousness, Matter and Miracles*, Carlsbad, California, Hay House Publishing, 2016

Chapter 25 (May the Force be with You)

Dyer, Dr. Wayne, *The Power of Intention*, Carlsbad, California, Hay House Publishing, 2005

https://starchild.gsfc.nasa.gov/docs/StarChild/questions/question30.html

Lipton, Bruce, *The Biology of Belief: Unleashing the Power of Consciousness, Matter and Miracles*, Carlsbad, California, Hay House Publishing, 2016

https://time.com/4854718/quantum-entanglement-teleport-space/

REFERENCES

Andrews, Ted, *Animal - Speak: The Spiritual & Magical Powers of Creatures Great & Small*, St. Paul, Minnesota, Llewellyn Publications, 2001

Clarke, Ardy Sixkiller, *Sky People: Untold Stories of Alien Encounters in Mesoamerica*, Newburyport, Massachusetts, Red Wheel, Weiser, 2014

Dyer, Dr. Wayne, *The Power of Intention*, Carlsbad, California, Hay House Publishing, 2005

Ingerman, Sandra & Wesselman, Hank, *Awakening to the Spirit World: The Shamanic Path of Direct Revelation*, Colorado, Sounds True Publishing, 2010

Lipton, Bruce, *The Biology of Belief: Unleashing the Power of Consciousness, Matter and Miracles*, Carlsbad, California, Hay House Publishing, 2016

McIntyre, Cathryn, *The Thoreau Whisperer: Channeling the Spirit of Henry David Thoreau*, Amazon Digital Services, 2018

Moskowitz, Kathy Strain, *Giants, Cannibals & Monsters: Bigfoot in Native Culture,* British Columbia, Hancock House Publishers, 2008

Tata, John, *The Boy from Plastic City*, Magnolia, Massachusetts, Fellow Pilgrim Books, 2016

Tompkins, William Mills, *Selected by Extraterrestrials*, South Carolina, Createspace 2010

Villoldo, Dr. Alberto, PH.D, *One Spirit Medicine: Ultimate Ways to Ultimate Wellness*, Carlsbad, California, Hay House Publishing, 2015

Villoldo, Dr. Alberto, *Shaman, Healer, Sage,* New York, Penguin, Random House Publishing, 2000

ABOUT THE AUTHOR

Ronny LeBlanc is a globally recognized figure in the world of paranormal, Bigfoot and UFOs. Ronny has been featured on Animal Planet's "Finding Bigfoot", "In Search of Monsters" and stars in Travel Channel's brand new series EXPEDITION BIGFOOT which premieres December 8th, 2019.
.
Ronny is an independent researcher, screenwriter and author of the critically-acclaimed and best-selling book Monsterland: Encounters with UFOs, Bigfoot and Orange Orbs, which details the history and connection between the various phenomena, highlighting his experience and a research area called Monsterland in central Massachusetts.

Ronny was the first person ever to cast a Bigfoot print in the Bay State from a trackway discovered by a couple in Leominster State Forest in the summer of 2010.
He is a regular speaker at the Exeter UFO Festival, New England UFO Conference and ParaFest and has been featured on nationally syndicated radio programs like Coast to Coast AM with George Noory, Fade to Black with Jimmy Church and was recently highlighted for his research in a cover story in The Boston Herald.

To learn more go to **www.RonnyLeBlanc.com**

EXPEDITION BIGFOOT – THE TRAVEL CHANNEL 2019

AUTHOR RONNY LEBLANC

The monsterland podcast

Made in the USA
Coppell, TX
03 January 2020